Between Heaven and Hell

A DIALOG SOMEWHERE BEYOND DEATH WITH
JOHN F. KENNEDY, C. S. LEWIS & ALDOUS HUXLEY

EXPANDED EDITION

PETER KREEFT

IVP Books

An imprint of InterVarsity Press
Downers Grove, Illinois

InterVarsity Press
P.O. Box 1400, Downers Grove, IL 60515-1426
World Wide Web: www.ivpress.com
E-mail: email@ivpress.com

Second edition ©2008 by Peter Kreeft

First edition ©1982 by InterVarsity Christian Fellowship of the United States of America

InterVarsity Press® is the book-publishing division of InterVarsity Christian Fellowship/USA®, a student movement active on campus at hundreds of universities, colleges and schools of nursing in the United States of America, and a member movement of the International Fellowship of Evangelical Students. For information about local and regional activities, write Public Relations Dept., InterVarsity Christian Fellowship/USA, 6400 Schroeder Rd., P.O. Box 7895, Madison, WI 53707-7895, or visit the IVCF website at <www.intervarsity.org>.

"The Apologist's" from POEMS by C. S. Lewis, copyright ©1964 by the Executors of the Estate of C. S. Lewis and renewed 1992 by C. S. Lewis Pte. Ltd., reprinted by permission of Harcourt Inc.

Design: Cindy Kiple
Images: Joe DeVelasco

ISBN 978-0-8308-3480-8

Printed in the United States of America ∞

Library of Congress Cataloging-in-Publication Data
Kreeft, Peter.
  Between heaven and hell: a dialog somewhere beyond death with John
F. Kennedy, C.S. Lewis and Aldous Huxley / Peter Kreeft.—Expanded
ed., 2nd ed.
    p. cm.
Includes bibliographical references and index.
  ISBN 978-0-8308-3480-8 (pbk.: alk. paper)
  1. Lewis, C. S. (Clive Staples), 1898-1963—Fiction. 2. Kennedy,
John F. (John Fitzgerald), 1917-1963—Fiction. 3. Huxley, Aldous,
1894-1963—Fiction. 4. Authors—Fiction. 5. Presidents—Fiction. 6.
Imaginary conversations. I. Title.
PS3561.R3817B4 2008
813'.54—dc22

                                                        2008005932

| **P** | 22 | 21 | 20 | 19 | 18 | 17 | 16 | 15 | 14 | 13 | 12 | 11 | 10 | 9 | 8 | 7 | 6 | 5 | 4 | 3 | 2 | 1 |
| **Y** | 26 | 25 | 24 | 23 | 22 | 21 | 20 | 19 | 18 | 17 | 16 | 15 | 14 | 13 | 12 | 11 | 10 | 09 | 08 |

For the Rev. Theodore J. Jansma

who kindled my knowledge of C. S. Lewis,

energized my knowledge of myself

and deepened my knowledge of Christ

Contents

Prologue

On November 22, 1963, three great men died within a few hours of each other: C. S. Lewis, John F. Kennedy and Aldous Huxley. All three believed, in different ways, that death was not the end of human life. Suppose they were right and suppose they met after death. How might the conversation go?

It would be part of "The Great Conversation" that has been going on for millennia. For these three men represented the three most influential philosophies of life in our human history: ancient Western theism (Lewis), modern Western humanism* (Kennedy) and ancient Eastern pantheism (Huxley).

These three men also represented the three most influential versions of Christianity in our present culture: traditional, mainline or orthodox Christianity (what Lewis called "mere Christianity"), modernist or hu-

---

*A word about the term *humanism*. It can be used in three different ways. (1) In its broadest sense, as an inheritance from ancient Greece and Rome, it signifies the importance and value of Man, especially as over against Nature. In this sense it is not only compatible with traditional biblical theism but is an ingredient in it. (2) In its narrowest sense, as a product of modern secularism and atheism, especially from the French Revolution, it signifies Man taking the place of God. In this sense it is not only incompatible with theism but its archenemy. (3) But the term is also often used in a third, middle sense, also distinctively modern: as an emphasis on Man rather than God; "horizontal" social activity rather than "vertical" religious experience; and religion without revelation, the supernatural, dogma, miracles, mystery or authority. This is the sense used here.

manistic Christianity (Kennedy), and Orientalized or mystical Christianity (Huxley).

Lewis took his Christianity straight, or "mere." Instead of reinterpreting Christianity in the light of any other tradition, ancient or modern, Eastern or Western, he interpreted those traditions in the light of Christianity. Following the lead of the medieval Christian philosophers in this way, he used much of ancient Western culture, especially Plato and Aristotle, as an aid for his Christian apologetics.

Kennedy, though not a philosopher or theologian, was probably in a vague and general way a humanistic Christian in the sense defined above. Although he did not give public expression to his personal religious beliefs (which is itself a humanistic rather than traditional attitude: relegating religion to private life), there is good evidence for this classification of Kennedy. (Much of it is presented in Gary Wills's *Bare Ruined Choirs.*) In any case, I take the literary liberty of supposing Kennedy to have been a typical modernist Christian in order to set up this complete and typical threesome. The purpose of the dialog is not historical accuracy; the *argument* is all, as it is with Plato's Socrates.

The fact that Lewis was a Protestant (an Anglican) and Kennedy a Roman Catholic is irrelevant here. Traditionalist and modernist Christians exist in both churches, and the difference between them is far more important than the difference between Protestantism and Catholicism. Whether the Pope speaks infallibly *ex cathedra* and whether there are seven sacraments or two are far less important than whether Jesus is literally divine and literally rose from the dead.

Our third man, Aldous Huxley, expressed his deepest religious beliefs in an anthology of mystical wisdom, *The Perennial Philosophy,* though he is better known for his novels. Like Kennedy, he sometimes used Christian categories to hold a different substance, rather than, like Lewis, using Greek or modern categories to hold Christian substance. In Huxley's case the substance was pantheism, and he reinterpreted Christianity as a form of the universal, "perennial" philosophy of pantheism. In historical fact, Huxley's Gnosticism was closer to the heart of his religion than his pantheism; but once again I take literary liberties of emphasis for the sake of the argument in the dialog.

The events of November 22, 1963, almost seem to have been providentially rigged to set up the situation I have imagined in this dialog: a microcosm of humanity's tripartite intellectual history as well as of the current tripartite debate among Christian theologians. The trialog centers on the Center, the hinge of our history: its main question is the identity of Jesus.

THE DIALOG

Time: November 22, 1963

Place: Somewhere beyond death

Characters: C. S. Lewis, Theist
John F. Kennedy, Humanist
Aldous Huxley, Pantheist

Kennedy: Where the hell are we?

Lewis: You must be a Catholic!

Kennedy: You could tell by the accent, eh?

Lewis: Yes. I say—aren't you President Kennedy? How did you get here—wherever *here* is?

Kennedy: Ex-President, I think: I seem to have been assassinated. Who are you? And—to return to my first question—where the hell are we?

Lewis: I'm C. S. Lewis. I just died too, and I'm pretty sure you're wrong about the location. This place just feels too good to be hell. On the other hand, I didn't see any God, did you?

Kennedy: No.

Lewis: Then it can't be heaven either. I wonder whether we're stuck in limbo.

Kennedy: Ugh! Do you really think so?

Lewis: Actually, I think it more likely that it's purgatory, especially if we end up getting out of it and into heaven. I did a bit of speculating about such places as a writer, especially in *The Great Divorce*. I don't suppose you've read it? No . . . well . . . But surely you should be familiar with such concepts if you were a Roman Catholic.

One world at a time? *Kennedy:* Well . . . I was more of a modern Catholic; I never bothered about transcendental mysteries or mythology. I was too busy trying to take care of the world I lived in for escapist thinking. "One world at a time," as Thoreau put it.

Lewis: You can see now that you were wrong, can't you?

Kennedy: What do you mean?

Lewis: Why, first that it isn't mythology. It's real. Wherever we are, here we are, large as life. And second, that the rule *isn't* "one world at a time." Here we are in another world talking about our past life on earth. That's two worlds at a time by my count. And while we were on earth we could think about this world too; that's also two worlds at a time, isn't it? Finally, it's not escapism. In fact, *not* to have prepared for this journey while we were living on earth would have been escapism. Don't you agree?

Kennedy: Hmm . . . I suppose you're right. But look! Someone else is coming. Can you make out who it is?

Lewis: Why, it's Huxley! Aldous Huxley. Aldous, welcome. How did you get here?

Huxley: Same way you did, I'm sure. I just died. Oh, I say! Kennedy and Lewis! What good company to die in—or live in, whatever we're doing. Where is this place, anyway?

Kennedy: That's what we're trying to figure out. Lewis thinks it may be some sort of limbo or purgatory. I'm just hoping it's not hell.

Huxley: Well, you're both wrong. It's heaven. It *must* be heaven.

Kennedy: Why?

Huxley: Because *everywhere* is heaven, if only you have enlightened eyes.

Is heaven every- where?

Lewis: Even hell?

Huxley: Oh, this is going to be fun! Lewis, you've lost none of your cantankerous penchant for Socratic questioning, have you? I remember you made Oxford a regular hornets' nest when you debated back on earth, and now you've shipped your hornets to heaven. This is a nice challenge.

Lewis: Then reply to it. If everywhere is heaven, then either hell does not exist, or hell is part of heaven. Which way will you have it, Aldous?

Kennedy: Wait, please! Before you two take off, could you give me some assurances about this sort of debate? I was a debater too, but we politicians confined ourselves to the concrete and tangible. I'm not at all convinced you can do anything more than talk through your hat about things you've never seen.

Lewis: So you want an assurance that there is some method of really finding the truth about things we can't see.

The question of method: how can we know?

Kennedy: Yes. Before you take off, be sure you have a plane that can fly, and can get back to earth and land. Lewis, you said you wrote a book about heaven. How the hell—how in heaven's name—how on earth—do you know anything about heaven? Have you ever been there?

Lewis: Yes, indeed. I've been in and out of the back doors of both many times.

Huxley: You see, Mr. President . . .

Kennedy: Please call me Jack.

Lewis: That will be rather confusing. My friends called *me* Jack.

Huxley: Suppose we let rank have first choice. Would you mind if we called you Lewis?

Lewis: If you please. Clarity seems to be the thing here, not titles.

Huxley: Fine. Now Jack, Lewis meant that remark about heaven spiritually, not literally.

Kennedy: Oh, well, if that's all you mean . . .

Lewis: No, wait. Let's not get bogged down in the swamps of "spiritual senses." Let's use words as literally as we can. I have *not* been in either heaven or hell literally.

Kennedy: Fine. Then how can you possibly know anything about them?

Lewis: I've been told.

Kennedy: What? What do you mean?

Lewis: Do you know anything at all about Tibet?

Kennedy: Of course.

Lewis: Have you ever been there?

Kennedy: No.

Lewis: Then how do you know anything about it?

Kennedy: Oh, I see. I've been told. But that's *knowing* only if you *believe* what you've been told.

Lewis: Exactly. It's called "faith."

Kennedy: You just passively, uncritically believe?

Lewis: No, I believe for good reason, and then I explore my belief with good reason.

Kennedy: I certainly don't want to impugn your faith, but I think my faith is quite different from yours.

Lewis: How?

Kennedy: You're one of those theological conservatives, aren't you?

Lewis: That depends on what you mean by the label. I've always thought *liberal* and *conservative* were terms used not to think but to avoid thinking. You can classify *anything* as liberal or conservative, then simply declare yourself one or the other, and all your thought for the rest of your life can be a knee jerk.

Kennedy: Well, *fundamentalist,* then.

Lewis: What does *that* mean? Many people associate it with "No drinking, smoking or swearing." By that standard, I was *not* a fundamentalist.

Literal vs. poetic interpretation of the Bible

Kennedy: I guess I mean, Do you take everything in the Bible literally?

Lewis: Of course not. When Jesus says, "I am the door," I don't look for a knob on him.

Kennedy: And when he talks about heaven and hell, do you look for real angels and demons?

Lewis: Yes.

Kennedy: Why? Why not interpret that poetically?

Lewis: Because the speaker didn't mean it poetically.

Kennedy: How do you know that?

Lewis: It's just simple common sense. Look here: do you think anybody, either Jesus or any of his hearers, reached for a literal knob when he said, "I am the door"?

Kennedy: No.

Lewis: And when he talked about heaven and hell, do you think his hearers interpreted it poetically?

Kennedy: No. They probably weren't sophisticated enough.

Lewis: Was Jesus a good teacher?

Kennedy: Of course.

Lewis: Does a good teacher take into account his audience, and how they are likely to interpret his words?

Kennedy: Of course.

Lewis: And does a good teacher deliberately use poetic language when he knows his audience will misinterpret it and take it literally?

Kennedy: No.

Lewis: You see what follows then. He meant to be taken literally when he talked about the existence of heaven and hell.

They're real places. We will certainly go to one of them forever. It matters infinitely which. *That* is certainly what he
meant everyone to get out of his teaching about heaven.

Kennedy: So you really believe in a place with devils with
horns and hoofs and all? You, a twentieth-century man?

Lewis: As I wrote in one of my books, I'm not sure what the
time has to do with it, and I'm not particular about the horns
and hoofs.

Kennedy: But otherwise, yes?

Lewis: Yes.

Kennedy: Well, I find it a lot easier to believe in the goodness
of man than in the badness of God.

Lewis: The *badness* of God?

Kennedy: Yes; can you imagine a worse God than one who
claps human beings into hell for all eternity?

Lewis: Yes, I can imagine a much worse God than that.

Kennedy: What God?

Lewis: One who would put people in hell *who didn't deserve
it.* An unjust God. But the God I believe in is not only above
injustice, he's also above justice. He's pure love.

**Hell and
the God
of love**

Kennedy: Wonderful! Then there is no hell.

Lewis: That does not follow.

Kennedy: Why not? How could pure love create hell?

Lewis: I don't think God creates hell; I think we do, or perhaps evil spirits do.

Kennedy: But God puts you there.

Lewis: No again. We put ourselves there by free choice.

Kennedy: Why would anyone do that? Who would prefer hell

to heaven if it was up to our own free choice?

Lewis: Anyone who found God uncomfortable, unendurable. Anyone who couldn't stand the light, the truth.

Kennedy: You mean it's not a matter of good deeds versus bad deeds, a kind of moral bookkeeping?

Lewis: No indeed. Look at the thief on the cross. He made it to paradise even though his life's red ink certainly outweighed the black.

Kennedy: I never thought of our destiny in any other terms than moral bookkeeping.

Lewis: That's why you never believed in hell.

Kennedy: Perhaps so. But I still don't understand how anyone could prefer hell to heaven.

Lewis: What do you think hell is? And what do you think heaven is?

Kennedy: As I just told you, I never gave it much thought. I suppose I thought of them in the usual way, as rewards and punishments, pleasures and pains, bliss and misery.

Could anyone choose hell?

Lewis: And you couldn't understand why anyone would freely prefer misery to bliss.

Kennedy: Exactly.

Lewis: Suppose the bliss is not a reward tacked onto a good life, like a grade tacked onto a school course, but the good life itself in its consummation. And suppose the punishment is also not external and tacked on but internal: the consummation of the evil itself. Do you see what follows?

Kennedy: I think so. We choose heaven or hell *in* every choice of good or evil.

Lewis: Exactly.

Kennedy: So that's what you meant by having been in heaven many times. But now you're interpreting the biblical heaven and hell poetically, not literally. Instead of golden streets and fire and brimstone, instead of physical rewards and punishments, your heaven and hell are spiritual states. I thought you insisted on interpreting heaven and hell literally.

Lewis: Their *existence* has to be taken literally, just as God's existence does. But their *nature* can only be grasped by symbols, just as God's nature can only be grasped by symbols.

Kennedy: That sounds more like my modernism than your traditionalism.

Lewis: If you knew the writings of the saints and mystics, you would know that my interpretation is quite traditional. You modernists tend to dismiss tradition without much of a hearing for it, you know.

Kennedy: I'm still not convinced that an ordinary, sane human being could end up in hell.

Lewis: Read my friend Charles Williams's novel *Descent into Hell* and you will be.

Kennedy: And where am I to find a bookstore in this place?

Lewis: Heh! Touché. Score one for you. I do tend to get rather absent-minded at times.

Kennedy: Well, let's get present-minded. To return to my original question, where are we? And why are we here, if this is neither heaven nor hell?

Huxley: Perhaps this is a second chance.

Lewis: I rather think it's the place and time to become clear   **Purgatory?**
about our first chance.

Kennedy: What do you mean by that? What first chance?

Lewis: The choices we already made on earth.

Kennedy: I thought you said you thought this was purgatory?

Lewis: I do. What do *you* mean by purgatory?

Kennedy: You do love your questions, don't you?

Huxley: He's Socrates reincarnated, Jack.

Lewis: Forget the compliment and answer the question, if you please—that is, if you really want to find out where we are and what we're supposed to be doing. You see, I'm not sure either, and I'm asking these questions to clarify my own ideas and find the truth, not just to win a debate with you or to teach you something that I know and you don't.

Kennedy: Aldous was right. You do sound like Socrates. All right, I'll try to answer your question. What do I mean by purgatory? I never thought much about it. But most Catholics believed it was a place where you had to go to suffer for your sins. What do you think?

Remedial reading of life

Lewis: I suspect that idea is not wholly wrong, but not wholly right either. I think it's more likely that purgatory is a place for education rather than suffering—a sort of "remedial reading" of your earthly life. As such, it's really the first part of heaven, not a distinct place. So I think we are being prepared for deep heaven if this is purgatory.

Kennedy: I hope you're right.

Lewis: Why? Are you afraid we're in the other place?

Kennedy: Frankly, I'm not as bothered by the possibility of being in hell as I am by your belief in hell. I find the first quite remote, but the second quite present and threatening.

Lewis: Why do you find my belief in hell threatening if you don't find hell itself threatening?

Kennedy: For the same reason you'd find belief in witches threatening even if you didn't believe in witches.

Lewis: I see. Does it bother your mind or your emotions?

Kennedy: What do you mean?

Lewis: I mean, are you bothered by my intellectual error, or by my motives for believing it?

Kennedy: The second.

Lewis: I thought so.

Kennedy: How could a good and reasonable and kind man like you want to believe in a place of eternal torment? Are you a closet sadist?

Lewis: If a mother shouts to her baby to run out of the street because a truck is coming, is she a sadist?

Kennedy: Of course not.

Lewis: But she believes in the truck and the threat it poses.

Kennedy: Yes, but she doesn't want it to threaten her baby. She doesn't make up a scary thing like that.

Lewis: Precisely. And we don't want hell to exist. We didn't make it up.

Kennedy: Why do you believe it then?

Lewis: It's a doctrine of faith. The church has always taught it. The Bible teaches it. Jesus clearly taught it.

Kennedy: So you accept this terrible thing on faith.

Lewis: Yes.

Kennedy: Simply because you've been told.

Lewis: At first, yes. But then, investigating what I've been told—what *we've* been told, Jack—with my mind and my imagination, I find that it commends itself to my reason and invites exploration by my rational imagination.

Kennedy: "Faith seeking understanding."

Lewis: Yes. It's a very old enterprise. Augustine, Aquinas, Dante, Milton . . .

Kennedy: But you begin with faith.

Lewis: Yes.

Faith, reason and authority

Kennedy: And you believe in the first place simply on the grounds of authority, and only later try to prove some of it.

Lewis: Yes.

Kennedy: In other words, you give up your mind to the church.

Lewis: No, for two reasons. Not my mind first of all but my will, and not to the church first of all but to God. But the God to whom I say "Thy will be done" replies, "It is my will that you believe what I have revealed to you."

Kennedy: Through the church?

Lewis: Through the church and the Scriptures, whatever their proper interrelationship. I'd rather not go into the whole Protestant-Catholic question now.

Kennedy: Why? To avoid hurting anyone's feelings?

Lewis: My goodness, no. I hope we're all at least mature enough not to have to worry about *that*. We're trying to find the truth, not put each other down.

Kennedy: Why, then?

Lewis: For two reasons. First, whenever I wrote any apologetics back on earth, I carefully avoided that question because I believed God had put me to work on the front lines, where Christianity faces the world, not behind the lines, where a civil war rages among Christians. My business was to defend "mere Christianity," not any one particular church. Second, because we two are not representative samples: I'm more Catholic than most Protestants, especially concerning church, tradition and authority; and you're more Protestant than most Catholics, de-emphasizing just those things—if I'm not mistaken.

Kennedy: No, you're not mistaken. And I think we ought to argue about authority as such rather than about hell, because it's on the grounds of authority that you believe in hell—and many other things as well.

Lewis: Fine.

Kennedy: I feel I'm really sticking my neck out, though, debating with a professional theologian.

Lewis: I'm *not* a professional theologian. But real debate, debate to unearth the truth, not to beat your opponent, seems to be the right thing to do here—as if we were brought here just for that purpose. Do you have that feeling too?

Kennedy: Yes, very strongly.

Lewis: Aldous, we've been leaving you out. Do you have the same feeling?

Huxley: Yes, and I'd like to keep listening for a while, if it's all right with you. As far as authority goes, I think I'm on Jack Kennedy's side; but I'm with you, Lewis, in being a traditionalist. My tradition, however, is broader than yours. It includes the whole of what I call "the perennial philosophy". . .

Lewis: Thereby stealing an epithet from the medieval Christians . . .

Huxley: Who don't deserve exclusive rights to it! The truly perennial philosophy goes back to the Hindu Vedas. But I'd like to hold my own trump card for a while and see how Jack fares against you, Lewis. I'll jump in later, on Jack's side, I'm pretty sure.

Lewis: I'm doubly pleased: that you both will *debate* with me and that you *both* will debate with me.

The plan of debate

Kennedy: Aren't you cowed by the odds? Two against one.

Lewis: The odds always favor the truth.

Huxley: Beware this man, Jack. No one has ever cowed him in debate. He's a Chesterton, a Shaw.

Lewis: Thank you, but the comparison is inaccurate on two counts.

Huxley: There he goes again!

Lewis: First, Shaw and Chesterton were giants; second, they were *wits.* I'm neither.

Kennedy: What are you, then?

Lewis: Just a plain Christian trying to think clearly.

Huxley: See, Jack? He's a Socrates. Mock humility!

Lewis: Not mock.

Huxley: So you're really humble, eh? And proud of it, no doubt?

Kennedy: Could you Britishers stop the badinage and start the debate? I'm anxious to hear Lewis's defense of authority.

Huxley: Go ahead, Lewis. I promise to be the silent audience for a while.

The Christian authority: Christ

Lewis: Please jump in whenever you like. Well, now, I'd rather not defend authority in general, only the authority on which I believe in heaven and hell, which was the question we began with. That authority is the authority of Jesus Christ. It's not *authority* but *Christ* that is the center of my faith, and if we ever get out of this place and into heaven, he will be our way out and in. So the issue of Christ has the primacy, both theoretically and practically.

Kennedy: I believe in Christ too, but I'm not comfortable with the concept of authority in relation to him. Didn't he say his only authority was love?

Lewis: Where is he recorded as having said that?

Kennedy: Well . . . something like that, anyway. The point is, I'm a Christian too, but a different sort than you, and I think a more mature sort—one who doesn't need as much reliance on authority as you do. Perhaps if you had ever been a president you would have come to be suspicious of authority too.

Lewis: Weren't you suspicious of authority *before* you came to acquire it?

Kennedy: Well . . . yes.

Lewis: Why are you suspicious of authority?

Kennedy: Because it sounds like a cop-out, a handing over your mind to someone else, a blind leap in the dark, a security blanket, a return to the womb. It's the easy way out to let someone else tell you what to think.

Suspicion of authority

Lewis: Do you really think that's the motive for my acceptance of the authority of Christ?

Kennedy: I don't claim to judge you and your motives personally, Lewis, but those seem to me in general the motives for authoritarianism, yes.

Lewis: Let's let that pass for a moment, rather than delving into psychoanalysis. Let's just suppose that those *were* my motives (which I do not grant); do you conclude from this that my old-fashioned beliefs are not true?

Kennedy: If you only believe them for those reasons, yes.

Lewis: Isn't that the genetic fallacy?

Huxley: That means determining the truth or falsity of an idea by its origin, its genesis.

Kennedy: I knew that. You know, I went to Harvard. Not everything west of Oxford is Yahoo territory.

Huxley: Sorry. Just trying to help.

Lewis: Well? *Haven't* you committed the genetic fallacy?

Kennedy: Frankly, I'm not sure it's a fallacy. If I believed something without good reason, isn't that sufficient grounds for your discounting my belief?

Lewis: But that's not *disproving* it. An idea is false only because it fails to correspond to reality, and true only because it does correspond to reality, not because of its psychological origin. I might arrive at a true idea by nonrational means.

Kennedy: So you admit authority is irrational.

Lewis: No, I don't. I may have good reason for trusting my authority.

Kennedy: I also dislike your simple definition of the truth of an idea. I don't think you can define truth in any simple way, like "correspondence to reality." All sorts of problems lie sleeping in those polysyllabic abstractions.

Lewis: Shall I put it into even simpler, concrete words of one syllable?

Kennedy: What?

Lewis: Truth.

Kennedy: You mean you will define truth in words of one syllable?

What is truth? A simple answer

Lewis: Exactly. It's not my invention by any means. It goes back to Aristotle, and it's not at all difficult.

Kennedy: All right, let's hear this nondifficult definition of truth in words of one syllable.

Lewis: Here it is. If one says of what is that it is, or of what is not that it is not, he speaks the truth; but if one says of what is that it is not, or of what is not that it is, he does not speak the truth.

Kennedy: That's amazing!

Lewis: But true.

Kennedy: Why, yes it is. A masterpiece of simplicity.

Lewis: I'm glad to see you recognize genius. *And* truth.

Kennedy: But even if I know what truth is, I still don't know why the genetic fallacy is a fallacy.

Lewis: Because a true idea can still have a nonrational cause.

Kennedy: Give me an example.

Lewis: Gladly. Most people in the Middle Ages accepted the two ideas that the earth was round and that the universe was enormously large simply because of the authority of Ptolemy, just as they accepted the idea that the sun revolved around the earth rather than the earth around the sun because of Ptolemy, not because they proved it for themselves. Yet the first two ideas were true, even though the third was false.

Kennedy: Wait a minute. Isn't that a false example? Didn't everyone think the earth was flat in the Middle Ages? And that the universe was tiny and cozy? Wasn't it modern science that opened up the universe and made it so difficult to believe in a providential divine plan for this little out-of-the-way planet?

Lewis: Sorry, Jack, but you're simply misinformed about that. Most of the modern world is, you know. Nearly every schoolboy is taught what you've been taught, and it's simply not true.

Kennedy: Can you prove that?

Lewis: Yes. Read Ptolemy's *Almagest,* book I, section 5. It's *the* authoritative astronomy text that everyone accepted in the Middle Ages.

Kennedy: That's quite a shock, and I went to Harvard. At any rate, the point of this example of yours is . . . ?

Lewis: That you can't decide whether an idea is true or false simply by knowing whether someone accepts it for a rational or a nonrational reason. Even if you think authority is a nonrational motive for accepting an idea, the idea may still be true, as Ptolemy's first two ideas were.

Kennedy: Of course. I see. But it still seems right to be suspicious of your easy reliance on authority. I think you do that because you need an intellectual security blanket—a substitute mother, perhaps. Didn't you lose yours early in life?

Lewis: Yes, and I could equally argue that you hate authority because you rankled under your authoritarian father. You see, two can play at that game, and the personal suspicions simply cancel each other out. We're left with the objective issue.

Kennedy: Let's get down to that, then. Justify arguing from authority.

Human vs. divine authority

Lewis: I want to distinguish first between human and divine authority. Although I'm respectful of human authority, I don't want to argue from it as an unquestioned premise. It was a cliché among the medieval philosophers . . .

Kennedy: Those authoritarians!

Lewis: Quite the contrary. The cliché was "The argument from authority is the weakest of arguments."

Kennedy: The *medievals* said that?

Lewis: Yes. They were quite rational, contrary to the popular superstition about them.

Kennedy: What did they mean by authority?

Authority not power

Lewis: Not what most people mean today, power. Obviously, the use of power to settle an argument is a fallacy. It's called the *argumentum ad baculum,* the "argument from the big stick." The argument from authority may be a weak argument, but it's an argument, not a fallacy, because authority doesn't mean power.

Kennedy: What does it mean?

Lewis: The root meaning is "right, based on origin." It is the author who has authority, author's rights. The authority of Christ (which is what we're supposed to be talking about) is based on his identity as the divine Author of the world. The Author entered the story as one of his characters.

Kennedy: That's just what I can't buy: that old-fashioned theology of God descending from heaven like a meteor.

Lewis: All right, then, let's be very specific. Who is Jesus, according to your faith?

Kennedy: The ideal man, the man so perfect and wise that his followers called him divine. Not God become man but man become God.

Lewis: A very nicely put summary of humanist Christology; but do you think this is *Christianity?*

Kennedy: Old Christianity, no; New Christianity, yes. The only form of it a modern man can believe without giving up his intellectual honesty. I heard a preacher put it this way: you can be honest, or intelligent, or a medieval-style Christian, or any two of the three, but not all three. Work that out for yourself.

Lewis: Very clever, but the same barb can be used to sting anyone. I can say you can be honest, or intelligent, or a modernist, or any two of the three, but not all three. The substantive point; as distinct from the debater's nicety, is the identity of Jesus. Let's zero in on that issue.

Kennedy: Fine. Who is Jesus?

Lewis: God become man.

Author's rights

Jesus: God become man or man become God?

Old Christianity vs. New Christianity

Kennedy: Literally?

Lewis: Yes.

Kennedy: How can you as an educated twentieth-century man take such an outdated position?

Lewis: As distinct from your new, modern one?

Kennedy: Yes.

Lewis: Because for one thing, your new position is as old as the hills. Or, at least, as old as Arius.

Kennedy: Who?

New Christianity, a very old heresy

Lewis: Arius, a fourth-century heretic who carried half the church with him even after the Council of Nicea addressed the issue by clearly and strongly affirming Jesus' divinity. The same thing is happening again today with modernism and humanism. Your so-called new Christianity is nothing but the old Arian heresy in new dress.

Kennedy: Really, now, there's no need to call each other names.

Lewis: I didn't call you a name; I just labeled your position accurately.

Kennedy: I wish you would avoid using labels like *heretic.*

Lewis: I used the label *heresy,* not *heretic.* The position, not the person.

Kennedy: I see. The "love the sinner, hate the sin" distinction.

Lewis: Quite.

Kennedy: I still wish we could avoid that label.

Lewis: Why?

Kennedy: It's . . . so . . . so outdated. So unenlightened. So medieval. So primitive.

Lewis: Jack, do you tell time with an argument?

Kennedy: What?

Lewis: I said, do you tell time with an argument?

Kennedy: What in the world do you mean by that?

Lewis: When you want to know what time it is, what do you look at? An argument or a clock?

Kennedy: A clock, of course.

Lewis: And what do you use an argument for, if not to tell time?

Kennedy: Why, to prove something, of course. Or to try to.

Lewis: Something false or something true?

Kennedy: Something true.

Lewis: So you tell time by the clock and truth by an argument.

Kennedy: Among other means, yes.

Lewis: Not vice versa?

Kennedy: No.

Lewis: But you were trying to tell truth by the clock a minute ago.

Kennedy: Truth by the clock?

Telling the truth with the clock

Lewis: When *I* want to disprove an idea, I try to prove that it is *false*. *Your* argument against my idea that your belief was a heresy was simply that my idea was *old*. *Outdated,* I believe you said. *Medieval* and *primitive* were two more of your terms. Those are all clock words, or calendar words. (Calendars are only big, long clocks, after all.)

Kennedy: I see Aldous did well to warn me against you! All right, my friend. If you want to be so logical, I challenge you: prove to me logically that Jesus is God and not just man.

Lewis: All right.

Kennedy: What?

Lewis: I just said, "All right." Why the surprise?

Kennedy: I thought you were going to say something about mysteries and faith and authority and the church. Do you mean you are going to try to *reason* yourself into the old faith?

Lewis: Not myself; I'm already there. But you, perhaps.

The role of reason in faith

Kennedy: Did you reason yourself into it? Did you arrive at your belief by reason alone?

Lewis: Reason *alone?* Of course not. But I looked before I leaped. I reasoned before I believed. And after I believed too—I mean, once I believed, I was convinced by the way reason backed up faith. It couldn't prove *everything,* but it could give strong arguments for many things, and it could answer all objections.

Kennedy: All objections?

Lewis: Certainly.

Kennedy: That sounds pretty arrogant to me. Who are you to answer all objections?

Lewis: No, no, I don't claim that *I* can answer all objections but that *reason* can—that all objections are answerable.

Kennedy: Why do you believe that?

Lewis: If truth is one, if God is the author of all truth, both the truth of reason and the truth of faith (I mean divine revelation), then there can never be a rational argument against faith that's telling, that's unanswerable. Faith may go beyond reason but it can never simply contradict reason.

Faith in reason

Kennedy: That's a very unusual position, you know. Such a faith in reason!

Lewis: Justin Martyr, Clement of Alexandria, St. Augustine, St. Anselm, St. Thomas Aquinas . . .

Kennedy: What is this? A roll call?

Lewis: Just a few names from the past who teach this "very unusual position." It was the mainline position for over a thousand years, before the modern loss of faith in everything, including reason.

Kennedy: I'm simply flabbergasted. I find myself face to face with a dinosaur.

Lewis: Are you going to argue by the clock again?

Kennedy: No. I'll duel with your weapons, logic. Argue away!

Lewis: They're not my weapons. Logic is nobody's possession. We have absolutely equal rights in that field, Mr. President.

Kennedy: Another point for you. I knew it was suicide to argue with a debater.

Lewis: The point is not for *me,* Jack, but for truth. The whole point of debating, for me, is not for me or you to win but for truth to win; not to see *who's* true but to see *what's* true. In fact, I won't "argue away" unless you're with me on this.

Kennedy: I am.

Lewis: Good. I knew I had an honest man here.

Kennedy: Of course.

Lewis: No, not "of course." Honesty is very hard, and very rare, and very precious.

Kennedy: I have to agree. I know enough psychology to know that the mechanisms of self-deception are very, very clever. But let's get down to the substantive argument you promised. You said you would prove Jesus was divine.

I. The main argument

The most important argument in Christian apologetics

Lewis: Yes. The argument is not original with me. In fact, most of my thinking and writing isn't; I'm a dwarf standing on the shoulders of giants, as the medievals put it. That's the key to far-sighted vision: good teachers. My teachers here are some of the early Christians, and this was one of the first arguments they used in their apologetics. I think it is the single most important argument in all of Christian apologetics.

Kennedy: Why?

Lewis: Because it proves the divinity of Christ; and that is the centrally important doctrine for two reasons.

Kennedy: Namely?

(1) The "skeleton key" principle

Lewis: First, the skeleton key principle: it opens all other doctrinal doors.

Kennedy: You mean once you believe that, anything goes?

Lewis: No, anything *he* says goes. Most orthodox Christians like myself believe all the doctrines of their faith not on the basis of their own reasoning or experience of each separate doctrine (at least not at first; reason and experience may confirm them, or some of them, later), but on the basis of the authority of Christ.

Kennedy: The Protestant thing, you mean? Just me and Jesus alone?

Lewis: That's a diversion, and not even an accurate one. A diversion from the "mere Christianity" we're discussing, and an inaccurate one because most Protestants don't limit religion or religious authority to "me and Jesus alone." They believe the authority of Christ comes to them through the Scriptures first and the church second, while Catholics reverse that order, arguing that the church wrote the Scriptures. But that's a diversion from our main point.

Kennedy: Yes. You spoke of *two* reasons why the divinity of

Christ is central. First was the skeleton key point. What's the second?

Lewis: The destiny of human life is at stake.

Kennedy: How?

Lewis: This is obviously an enormous point. I'll try to keep it short and simple. Let's begin with a basic principle of causality: you can't give what you don't have—or, whatever is in the effect must be in the cause. Do you agree with that principle?

It changes the meaning and destiny of human life.

Kennedy: Of course. I studied philosophy too, you know.

Lewis: I never underestimated your mind. Well, if Christ is not divine, he can't give divinity or divine life, can he?

Kennedy: No. But that's not his function. His function is to be the perfect human life.

Lewis: And in that case human destiny is simply to be human, not to be transformed, caught up into the movements of the dance of divinity-and-humanity in one.

Kennedy: Can you say that less poetically?

Lewis: Yes. Are we born to become big men or little gods?

Kennedy: I see the issue. But I'm basically a humanist; I view the idea of a human being attaining divinity as mythology, fit for an ancient Greek but not for a modern. No. I'm not arguing by the clock again, but you haven't proved that Jesus was divine yet.

Lewis: Not "was divine"; "is divine."

Kennedy: OK. A fine point of grammar.

Lewis: No, the point is crucial. It's not just a question of words, of proper tenses.

Kennedy: Explain.

Lewis: Divine life is immortal. A divine Christ is not dead; he is not in the dead past, but alive in the living present. I think the angels at the empty tomb on Easter morning were speaking not only to the women who were looking for Jesus' body, but to all modernist Christians like yourself down through the ages when they asked: "Why do you seek the living among the dead?"

Is Jesus alive now? *Kennedy:* I believe he is still alive, just as Socrates and Caesar and Lincoln are still alive—in the spirits of all their followers.

Lewis: Christianity insists on more. He is alive as you and I are alive. Just as really alive and present as I am.

Kennedy: Where is he, then? Show him to me.

Lewis: Do you think I keep him in my back pocket, that I can bring him out to show him at your beck and call?

Kennedy: Then how could you ever prove he is alive and immortal and divine? You are a mere man, reasoning with mere words about an invisible and absent person who died centuries ago.

Lewis: The question of *how* is another diversion. It's the whole issue of methodology. Most of philosophy for the last century has gotten hung up on that diversion, on "second-order questions," questions about questions, questions about how to prove things instead of questions about real things.

Kennedy: I think my question is an honest and legitimate one, and I demand an answer.

Lewis: The only answer is the proof itself. The only way to show that anything is possible and how it is possible, is to show that it is actual. The only way to prove that a thing can be proved is to prove it.

Kennedy: Prove it then. No more diversions.

Lewis: Aut deus aut homo malus.

Kennedy: What? Are we speaking in tongues now, or what?

Lewis: That's my proof, or its summary. It's Latin for . . .

Kennedy: I know. I was just kidding. "Either God or a bad man." Now how is that a proof?

Lewis: Let's go through the logic of it. The first premise is that Christ must be either God, as he claims to be, or a bad man, if he isn't who he claims to be. The second premise is that he isn't a bad man. The conclusion is that he is God.

The logic of *aut deus aut homo malus*

Kennedy: The logical form seems to be correct, but why must I accept either premise?

Lewis: As for the second premise, even his opponents do not usually say he was a *bad* man. They try to make out that he was only a good man whom his disciples "divinized." But the first premise states that "just a good man" is the one thing he could not possibly be.

Kennedy: Why? Prove the first premise. That's the nub of the argument. The second is a platitude.

Lewis: Right. Consider this: Christ *claimed* to be the "Son of God." Remember what that implies.

Proof of the first premise

Kennedy: What?

Lewis: What is the primary thing a father gives to his son?

Kennedy: Love, I suppose.

Lewis: Try again.

Kennedy: Education? Caring? Time?

Lewis: All those can be given only if the primary gift is given first.

Kennedy: You mean existence.

Lewis: Yes. And what kind of existence?

Kennedy: Human existence, of course.

Lewis: Yes. Human existence, human life, human nature. Human parents give *humanity* to their children. And what do oyster parents give to their oyster children?

Kennedy: Oyster nature.

Lewis: Brilliant deduction! And wolf parents give wolf nature to their wolf children. And Martian parents give Martian nature. So the son of an oyster is what?

Kennedy: An oyster.

Lewis: And the son of a wolf is . . .

Kennedy: A wolf. And the son of a Martian is a Martian.

Lewis: And the Son of God?

Kennedy: I see. The title does seem to imply divinity, doesn't it?

Huxley: You're giving in too easily, Jack. Actually, the term *son of God* is sometimes used in Scripture to refer to creatures. Angels are called sons of God in some places, and all Christians are called sons of God.

Lewis: Shall we review some of the other things Jesus said that more clearly claim divinity?

Kennedy: Before we look at that, I'd like to be clear about the logic of the argument. Suppose Jesus did claim divinity. That doesn't prove he was divine. Lots of people claim things that aren't theirs.

Lewis: But a mere man who claimed to be God would not be a good man, don't you see?

Kennedy: Hmmm. What would he be, according to your thinking?

Lewis: A bad man, just as the argument says.

Kennedy: Suppose he was just confused?

Lewis: Then he was intellectually bad. You see, he either believes his claim to be God, or he doesn't. If he does, then he is intellectually bad—very bad, in fact, because that's a pretty large confusion! And if he does *not* believe his claim, then he is morally bad: a deceiver and a terrible blasphemer.

Kennedy: So what are all the possibilities?

Lewis: An intellectually bad man, a morally bad man, a good man or God. In other words, insane, blasphemer, nice guy or God. And the one of those four that he couldn't possibly be is the third. But that's what you and millions of other humanists think he was.

Only four possibilities: Jesus is insane, blasphemer, "nice guy" or God.

Kennedy: The argument is just too neat. I simply can't stomach that kind of black-and-white thinking.

Lewis: That is an interesting psychological fact about your personal temperament, but it doesn't refute my argument, you know. You don't answer an argument by saying you don't like it, or don't like arguments, or can't stomach clarity.

Kennedy: It's not clarity I can't stomach. It's black-and-white thinking.

Black-and-white thinking

Lewis: Isn't the second just a poetic way of saying the first? What do you mean by black-and-white thinking if not clarity?

Kennedy: It just isn't relevant to the world. The real world is gray. There are no absolutes, no black or white.

Lewis: You didn't answer my question, but I'll let that pass. Apparently you do mean "clarity" by "black-and-white thinking." And to say "there are no absolutes" sounds like a pretty absolute statement. Finally, I think I can convince you that there *are* some things that are black or white.

Kennedy: I challenge you. Name one.

Lewis: I'll name two.

Kennedy: Really?

Lewis: Yes. Black, and white.

Kennedy: That's just a trick.

Lewis: No, it isn't. It's like the statement, "There are no absolutes." It contradicts itself. It can't be true.

Kennedy: But all those grays . . .

Lewis: What is gray but black and white combined?

Kennedy: But we're arguing about a person, not about colors. The illustration is not relevant.

Lewis: I agree.

Kennedy: What?

Lewis: I agree. You introduced it, not I.

Kennedy: What I want to say is this: how can you talk about a *person* in such stark, extreme alternative categories?

Extremism *Lewis:* With him, you have to. He forces you to one of two extreme positions by his claim, the most extreme claim anyone ever made.

Kennedy: Well, *I* don't feel forced into your extremes.

Lewis: Look here: suppose I claimed to be the greatest writer of the twentieth century. What would you think of me?

Kennedy: Why, that you were insufferably arrogant.

Lewis: Yes. But not quite insane?

Kennedy: Not necessarily.

Lewis: Now suppose I claimed to be the greatest human being who ever walked the earth—wiser than Solomon, more enlightened than Buddha, holier than any of the saints. What would you think of me then?

Kennedy: That you were an incredibly egotistical fool.

Lewis: A bit closer to insanity, right?

Kennedy: Probably well over the edge.

Lewis: Fine. Now suppose I claimed to be God—the God who created you and this whole universe, the cosmic Mind or *Logos* that has always existed. Suppose I claimed to be your Savior, to forgive your sins, save your soul from hell and take you to heaven if only you believed in me and worshiped me. Suppose I said I was utterly sinless, and that I would rise from the dead, and because I would rise, you would rise too. What would you think of me then?

Kennedy: If *you* said that?

Lewis: Yes.

Kennedy: That you were quite insane, if you really believed it. What's the principle you're trying to prove?

Lewis: That the difference between what you really are and what you claim to be is a measure of your insanity.

Kennedy: I see. Then it would have to work for claims to be less than you really are as well as more.

Lewis: It does. If I claimed to be the stupidest and wickedest man in the world, you would say I was suffering from a very severe inferiority complex. If I said I was really an ape, not a man, you would say I was insane. If I said I was a teakettle, you would think me even more insane. Correct?

Kennedy: Correct.

Lewis: And the gap between God and creatures is greater than any other gap, any gap between any two creatures, because it's infinite. Correct?

The gap between your claim and the truth, a measure of your insanity

Kennedy: Correct.

Lewis: So it follows that the greatest insanity would be claiming to be God.

Huxley: May I put in my two cents' worth here? I think I can bail you out, Jack. You see, the claim to be God is not as shocking as it sounds to you Westerners. In Hinduism . . .

Kennedy: Aldous, I wonder whether we could wait a bit before you give your Oriental interpretation of Jesus? I'd really like to hear it, but I *am* a Westerner and I want to finish the argument in Western terms first, before turning East with you.

Lewis: Good for you, Jack. I was hoping you'd have the guts to follow the argument.

Huxley: And I hope you will have the guts to follow my argument too when I give it, both of you.

Jesus' claims to divinity   *Kennedy:* I'm sure we both will. But Lewis, could you review for us some of the claims for divinity that Jesus made? I think we should get our data straight first, before interpreting it. What, exactly, did he say about himself?

Huxley: And did he really say it? There's another question: how reliable are the texts?

Lewis: Let's gather our data, by all means. What *did* he say? As to whether he really said it, Aldous, hadn't we better deal with the textual question separately? One thing at a time.

Kennedy: Yes, one thing at a time. But since both Aldous and I doubt the historical accuracy of the texts, either of us could jump into the textual question when it comes up. I think I'd rather let Aldous handle that as part of his argument. He knows more than I do about texts.

Lewis: All right, then. Taking the texts as they stand, let's gather the data. Here are some quotations: "I and the Father are one." "He who has seen me has seen the Father." "I am the resurrection and the life; he who believes in me, though he die, yet shall he live, and whoever lives and believes in me shall never die." "I am the bread of life." "I am the way, and the truth, and the life; no one comes to the Father but by me." "Your sins are forgiven."

Kennedy: Wait a minute. How is that last statement a claim to divinity? I'd want to forgive others' sins too. And didn't he command us to forgive one another?

Lewis: Yes, for sins against yourself. For instance, you just forgave Aldous for a little insult before about Yahoos and Harvard. But suppose you forgave him for insulting *me?*

Kennedy: That would be asinine.

Lewis: Quite. Do you see what it would be assuming?

Kennedy: Whoever forgives assumes he has the *right* to forgive.

Lewis: Yes, and who has the right to forgive an offender?

Kennedy: The one offended.

Lewis: Exactly. So Jesus' claim to forgive all sins assumed that he was the one offended in all sins. And who is that?

Kennedy: I see. God. The author of the moral law.

Lewis: And then there's the supreme claim to divinity, the cruncher: the sacred Tetragrammaton.

Kennedy: Sorry, you have me there; what's the sacred tetra-whatchamacallit?

Lewis: The sacred Tetragrammaton, the holy four letter word, the name no Jew ever spoke because it is the name of God, revealed to Moses by God himself according to Exodus 3:14. No one really knows how to pronounce it, because no one ever dared to pronounce it except God, and the whole word was not

"I AM"

written down, just the four consonants, the Tetragrammaton. Old English Bibles printed it *Jehovah,* and the newer ones print *Yahweh.* It means "I AM." And Jesus spoke it in John 8:58: "I tell you most solemnly, before Abraham was, I AM."

Kennedy: Aren't there many names for God in the Bible? What's so special about this one, that no Jew dares pronounce it?

Lewis: All the other names for God are *our* names for him; this one is his own revealed name for himself. All the other names tell what he is or does in relation to us: Creator, Redeemer, King and so on. But this one tells what he is in himself: the sheer, absolute act of being.

Kennedy: So out of respect no Jew would ever say it?

Lewis: More than respect. Respect is a human convention. This is a linguistic necessity inherent in that word and in no other. If God had said his name was anything else—Oscar, for instance, or X—we could utter his name without claiming to *be* God. I can say "Hello, Oscar" without claiming to be Oscar, or "X is Y" without claiming to be X. But to say "I AM" is to claim to *be* that "I." It's the purely first person name, private, subjective, unique.

Kennedy: I see. No one can say it except its owner.

Lewis: Yes. I can *express* a third person name, and I can *address* a second person name, but I can only *possess* the first person name.

Kennedy: Could you illustrate that?

Only two honest reactions to Jesus: worship or crucifixion

Lewis: I *express* in the third person when I say, "Oscar exists" or "X is good." I *address* in the second person when I say "O thou great Oscar" or "Dear X." But "I" is the one word we cannot ever express or address, only possess. Only I AM can say "I am." That's why those words were the most shocking thing ever uttered by a human tongue, and why the Jews who heard them tried to stone Jesus to death, and later succeeded in crucifying him. Death was the penalty for blasphemy according to the Mosaic Law. Theirs was a clear, honest reaction.

Kennedy: And mine is not?

Lewis: Frankly, no. They stared the terrible either-or in the face. You avoid it by avoiding "black-and-white thinking." But either this must be I AM himself speaking, or else a very, very bad man who deserved to be killed if anyone ever did, according to Mosaic Law.

Kennedy: A cruel law, from a cruel time. There's no need for us to be bound by it, and to call him worthy of execution.

Lewis: But we *would* call him worthy of incarceration. We would send for the men in the white coats instead of the executioners, wouldn't we, if we found a man who really, literally thought he was God? Would you call such a man good and wise?

Kennedy: Suppose not. Suppose he was insane. I don't really want to take the position that Jesus was insane—I'd like to say he was a good and wise man—but I don't know how to avoid your logic otherwise.

Lewis: Not *my* logic, remember? And why would you want to avoid it?

Kennedy: You have a penchant for asking uncomfortable questions. Well, just to complete the logic of your argument, can you prove your second premise, that Jesus was not a bad man, not insane?

Lewis: If I do, you know what follows, don't you?

Kennedy: What do you mean?

Lewis: Why, we've already proved the first premise: Jesus must be either God or a bad man. If we also prove the second

Proof of the second premise: Jesus' credibility

premise, that Jesus is not a bad man, then you must accept the conclusion that he is God.

Kennedy: I think I'm beginning to see why I want to avoid logic. But go on. Prove the second premise.

Lewis: All right, but the proof is not going to be a "black-and-white" one, as you might put it. It will depend on our intuitive understanding of human nature and human personality.

Kennedy: Sounds perilously vague and subjective to me.

Lewis: You were complaining a moment ago about my using the opposite kind of proof, a clear-cut, either-or, black-and-white argument. You're impossible to please!

Kennedy: It's just that I'm suspicious of some kinds of proof, in general.

Lewis: I see. You know, that's an easy way to avoid meeting a specific proof: impugning "that kind of proof in general" in a vague way. Wouldn't it be fairer to listen to the proof first? There just might be some very sound proofs that are based on intuition. How can you be sure this isn't one unless you look?

Kennedy: All right, I'm looking. What are you showing?

Human credibility detectors   *Lewis:* If you remember the Gospels, you remember that Jesus didn't come right out and claim divinity at first, clearly and unequivocally. He first let his disciples get to know him humanly. He appealed to their human credibility detectors.

Kennedy: Their what?

Lewis: That's the intuitive part. We all have innate, intuitive abilities to detect persons who are credible, or trustable, and those who are not.

Kennedy: I understand that.

Lewis: Jesus first established his human credibility with his disciples. Then he claimed divinity within that context of credibility. Thus, we must examine that context.

Kennedy: Why *must* we?

Lewis: To critically evaluate his claim to divinity.

Kennedy: Good. I certainly want to do that. A critical faith, not a blind faith; that's what I insist on.

Lewis: Fine. Now think: if you or I had claimed what he claimed, would anyone believe us?

Kennedy: Of course not.

Lewis: Then why did so many believe him?

Why did so many believe Jesus' incredible claim?

Kennedy: Perhaps they were just unenlightened, prescientific peasants.

Lewis: Have you ever heard the term *chronological snobbery?*

Huxley: May I interject something here? Let's turn the argument away from name calling. Paul of Tarsus certainly wasn't just a peasant, and Jack is certainly not a snob.

Kennedy, Lewis (together): That's not what we meant.

Huxley: In any case, let's try to answer Lewis's question "Why did so many believe Jesus?" by looking at a parallel case. Why did so many believe Guatama Buddha when he made an equally incredible claim?

Why did anyone believe Buddha's incredible claim?

Lewis: Good question (though I don't think his claim was *quite* as incredible as Jesus').

Huxley: And what's your answer, Jack?

Kennedy: It has to be the same as with Jesus: his human credibility.

Huxley: Do you realize—either of you—how incredible Buddha's claim was? Suppose I told you that I had just received the supreme enlightenment by sitting under a tree and eating a decent meal for the first time in years; that the content of that enlightenment was that all of us are living in total and perpetual illusion; that everything we think is real is really unreal, *sunyata,* emptiness—the world, the self, the body, the soul, the ego, the other; and that the only reality is *Nirvana,* "extinction," which *is neti . . . neti . . .* not this, not that, absolutely indescribable. Would you believe me if you heard that for the first time from me now?

Kennedy: Certainly not. I don't even believe it when I hear it from Buddha.

Lewis: So why *did* anyone believe it?

Huxley: Experience, my dear chap, experience. They experienced it for themselves. No authority, no divine revelation, no faith in Another, as you Christians appeal to so blindly.

Lewis: But Buddha's first disciples had not yet experienced Nirvana when they believed Buddha. Why did they believe in him? And many later generations of disciples first believe and only much later experience the Nirvana they believe in. Why would they find it unless they sought it? And why would they seek it unless they believed in it?

Kennedy: Then why *did* they believe it? Remember, this "it" is a *very* strange, almost unbelievable teaching.

Huxley: Certainly not on authoritarian grounds.

Lewis: Perhaps not on the authority of words or books or institutions, but it certainly *was* on the authority of Buddha himself, on his personality and its evident credibility.

Huxley: Well, yes. But I wouldn't like to call that *authority.* I'd call it *holiness.* Buddha was said to be "a man holy to his fingertips." If you had met him, you might have believed *anything* he said.

Lewis: Precisely. Whether we use the word *authority* for that or not is only a verbal quibble. But the word was used of Jesus too: "He taught as one who had authority, not as the Scribes." You've just agreed with my point, Aldous, though not with my terminology. Jesus' disciples believed what he said because they first believed him, just as Buddha's disciples believed what Buddha said because they first believed him.

Kennedy: But *we* never meet people like Jesus or Buddha. Is this really relevant to our experience?

Lewis: The principles of credibility are, surely. Let me give an example from one of my own books about an ordinary person, not someone like Jesus or Buddha. The situation is fictional, even fantasy; we would not experience it (though we can't be absolutely sure even of that, can we?). But the character in question is an ordinary girl. It's from *The Lion, the Witch, and the Wardrobe,* the first of the Chronicles of Narnia. Have either of you read it? No? Oh well, I didn't really think either of you would have time for serious things like children's fantasy. You were too busy with fantastic games like diplomacy and scholarship. (Half kidding, Jack. Put down that hand! Three-quarters kidding with you, Aldous. You can put away that scandalized look.)

Why did the Professor believe Lucy's claim of Narnia?

All right, then. The story begins with four English children playing hide-and-seek on a rainy day indoors in a large old country house owned by a wise old Professor Kirke. Lucy, the youngest, hides in a free-standing wardrobe in an empty room, and discovers that it has no back, but is an opening into a whole other world, Narnia. She goes through and has some adventures in Narnia, involving a faun and a wicked witch, before she finds her way back through the wardrobe. When she tells her brothers and sister about it, they all find only an ordinary wardrobe with a back. Naturally, they don't believe her, and she is in tears all day.

Finally, at supper, the Professor resolves the issue. He asks Peter, Lucy's oldest brother, How well do you know Lucy? (Quite well.) And how well do you know the universe? Are you *sure* such things can't possibly happen? Has science or history or experience proved its impossibility? (Well, no.) Why then it's quite plain: either Lucy is insane, or lying, or telling the truth. If you know her well enough to know she isn't insane or lying, and you don't know the universe well enough to be sure she couldn't possibly be telling the truth, you had better believe her. Simple logic. "What do they teach them in the schools nowadays, anyway?"

Kennedy: They teach them the real world, not fantasy. (Half kidding, Lewis.) I see your point. But surely you wouldn't believe someone if they came up to you with such a story. You'd think it much more likely that they were making it up, just as you made that whole story up. Things like that just don't happen in the real world. And neither do literal descents of the gods, or literal resurrections from the dead.

How do you know miracles can't happen?

Lewis: I might ask you what Professor Kirke asked Peter: How do you know that? Has science proved that miracles can't happen? But I've put that line of argument into another of my books, *Miracles* . . . No, I didn't think you had read it . . . and I'd rather follow out the psychological line of argument now. The point of my reference to Lucy was to show that like Lucy and like Buddha, Jesus says incredible things, and like Lucy and like Buddha, Jesus is a credible person. So we must either believe his unbelievable claim or disbelieve his believable personality, his personal credibility.

Kennedy: Let's examine his personality then, though I'm not sure where it will take us. I do know something about human nature, and human history, and great men of the past. I too wrote a book, you know, *Profiles in Courage.* No? You haven't read mine either? Well, we're even then. But go ahead with the argument.

Lewis: Let us divide all people into four categories . . .

Kennedy: Oh, oh. Here we go again. Black-or-white thinking.

Lewis: But surely there *are* categories. The only question is whether they are appropriate, fitting to the real.

Kennedy: I don't like divisions among people.

Lewis: But all categories are divisions, classifications, outlines.

Kennedy: Putting people into classes has done immense harm throughout human history.

Lewis: Really dividing people, yes. But not mentally dividing them. For instance, to mentally distinguish male and female is good, and necessary (how confused we would be if we couldn't, or wouldn't, as some seem to nowadays). But to really divide them, to isolate them, is usually bad. In fact, to unite them most fruitfully, you must mentally divide them most clearly: *vive la difference,* and all that.

Kennedy: I see that. But your classification is not going to be as obvious and natural as that, is it?

Lewis: Wait and see. Meanwhile, don't prejudge. You use categories too. For instance, you selected only great men, or men of great courage, rather than others, to write about in your book, thereby implicitly dividing people into two categories.

Kennedy: But it was a soft division, not a hard one. There was no simple black-or-white distinction between the courageous and the cowardly. Human qualities exist in degrees of gray, not in black or white.

Lewis: I agree.

Kennedy: What? You agree?

Lewis: Of course. Did you think my being logical somehow blinded me to reality?

Putting people into classes

Kennedy: Frankly, yes.

Lewis: Being *merely* logical blinds you to reality. Being merely *anything* blinds you to reality, because reality is not merely anything. Reality is everything.

Kennedy: Isn't there a special "mereness" to logic? It's pure form, with no content, but reality is content.

Lewis: Right. And this argument is about content, about real, living human personalities. That doesn't prevent the argument from having a logical form too.

Kennedy: Go on, then, divide. I'll suspend judgment until I see the result.

Divisions of humanity

Lewis: Thank you. Let's divide humanity first into the few enormously great and wise people like Jesus, Buddha, Socrates, Lao-Tzu, Moses, Muhammad, Confucius, Zoroaster . . .

Kennedy: I get you. You needn't go on with the list. But the dividing line between these few and the many is a soft one, not a hard one, you understand?

(1) Sages and non-sages

Lewis: I understand. Let's call these few the sages, and the vast majority of the human race that are left the non-sages. Although it is true, as you say, that the dividing line is soft, that sagacity is a matter of degree rather than a black-or-white quality, yet we can and do single out a few as extraordinarily sagacious, can we not?

Kennedy: Yes. But you had better define *sagacious* if you want your argument to be logical and objective rather than only a projection of your personal likes and dislikes.

Lewis: Quite right. I shall define and describe sagacity as soon as I finish my classification.

Kennedy: So far you have two classes. You said you were going to divide people into four.

Lewis: Yes. Let's also divide people into those who claim to be God and those who do not.

**(2)
Claimants
to divinity
and non-
claimants**

Kennedy: That's a strange division, but a clear one, I suppose, except for the term *God*.

Lewis: Yes. Let's confine ourselves to the God of the Bible.

Kennedy: Isn't that provincial?

Lewis: I don't mean *really* confining ourselves to the God of the Bible—though I'd argue that even that is not confinement or provinciality, just realism, because he's the only *real* God. But let that pass. I mean logically confining the definition of *God* to one of the many possible meanings of the term, for the sake of clarity.

Kennedy: I still think that's defining the term too narrowly.

Lewis: We don't want our terms to be ambiguous, do we?

Kennedy: No.

Lewis: And how do we avoid ambiguity?

Kennedy: By definition.

Lewis: And definition means confinement, doesn't it? *De-fino* and *con-fino* mean just about the same thing.

Kennedy: Yes.

Lewis: Then let us distinguish two classes of people: all those who claim to be the God the Bible talks about, and all those who do not.

Kennedy: Do you mean to say now that there is only one member to the first class? Only one man who claimed to be God? Is that going to be your point?

Lewis: Not at all. There are a number of such people, though you have probably never met one.

Kennedy: Where are they?

Lewis: Most of them are in insane asylums.

Insane Christs: the divinity complex

Kennedy: Oh. Yes. The "divinity complex."

Lewis: It is at least common enough to merit that technical term, and a paragraph or two in manuals of abnormal psychology. In fact, there was even a novel called *The Three Christs of Ypsilanti* about an insane asylum that had three people in it who claimed to be God in the flesh.

Kennedy: You realize, do you not, that your two classifications are very different? For one thing, the first is a matter of degree and the second is not.

Lewis: Correct. Sagacity is a matter of degree, but claiming literally to be God is not. So one of the dividing lines will be blurred and the other not. Now let's combine the two divisions and get our four classes of people:

First, there are those who neither claim to be God nor are remarkably sagacious: the vast majority of us.

Second, there are those who do not claim to be God and *are* remarkably sagacious: people like Buddha, Socrates, Confucius, Lao-Tzu, Moses, Muhammad and the rest.

Third, there are those who claim to be God and are not remarkably sagacious: the insane.

Fourth, there are those who both claim to be God and are remarkably sagacious.

Kennedy: And whom do you put into Class Four?

The uniqueness of Jesus

Lewis: Only one.

Kennedy: I thought so.

Lewis: Can you think of another?

Kennedy: No. But this classification alone does not prove Jesus' claim to divinity is true.

Lewis: No, but it amplifies and explains the premise of the *aut deus aut homo malus* proof. Only two kinds of men claim to be God, and one kind is a bad man, not a sage.

Kennedy: But you have not yet defined a sage. What is a sage, and what is a divinity complex, and why are the two incompatible? You must answer those three questions, or else I shall simply classify Jesus as a sage with a divinity complex.

Lewis: An insane sage? Isn't that almost a self-contradiction?

Kennedy: I need concrete definitions. Descriptions.

Lewis: Fine. Let's take your three questions one by one. First, **What is** what is a sage? You mean basically the same thing by *sage, guru,* **a sage?** *spiritual master, wise man, holy man* and so on, correct?

Kennedy: Yes.

Lewis: So do I.

Kennedy: Then define them.

Lewis: Sages seem to me all to have three prominent psycho- **(1) Wisdom** logical characteristics. First, unusual insight or wisdom.

Kennedy: About what? Anything? Is a great physical scientist a sage because he has insight into the workings of the atom?

Lewis: No. Insight into the human heart and character.

Kennedy: Good. I would define the wisdom of the sages in that human way too. How refreshing. I thought you were going to emphasize some abstract, speculative philosophical kind of wisdom.

Lewis: The sages *are* philosophers, but practical philosophers. Their insight includes both insight into universal truths about human nature—what you might loosely call philosophy—and insight into the peculiar truths and falsehoods of the individual —what you might call practical psychology.

Huxley: Buddhists call that combination *prajna.*

Lewis: It is not something that everyone has, is it?

Huxley: According to the Eastern sages, everyone has it but only the Enlightened release it, or wake up to it.

Lewis: In any case, it manifests itself only in the life of the sage.

Huxley: Correct.

Kennedy: Is there any objective way we non-sages can detect it?

Lewis: For one thing, it does not express itself in platitudes that everyone already knows. Sages seldom utter clichés. Their teaching is challenging, surprising, often upsetting. They make enemies by their wisdom.

Kennedy: I know what you mean. They are ahead of their times, pioneers, liberators.

Lewis: Why then do you think they are so unpopular? Why do they make enemies? Don't you believe people want to be liberated?

Kennedy: Well, yes, but . . . hmmm. That's a good question. What do you think?

Lewis: I think people *don't* want to be liberated. Not truly liberated, because that always involves pain.

Kennedy: Why?

Lewis: Because the one thing necessary for all true liberation is often very painful.

Kennedy: What's that?

Lewis: Truth.

Kennedy: But truth is a primary human need.

Lewis: Indeed. But we do not always want it. The sages tell

us the truths no one else tells us, the truths we need the most
and want the least.

Kennedy: And they are the pioneers, the progressives, the liberals who liberate.

Lewis: I don't think you can apply political categories to them.

Kennedy: But they *are* pioneers.

Lewis: Yes, but the radicals of one generation become the conservatives of the next. Their new teachings become the old truisms of their tradition, as the first roads to the American West became later superhighways.

Kennedy: A nice comparison. I'll keep my political categories in my back pocket for a little while. I'm not so sure they're totally unapplicable to the sages. They were public figures, after all. Anyway, what's your second characteristic of all sages?

Lewis: Love, altruism, compassion, selflessness.   **(2) Love**

Huxley: Prajna and *karuna*.

Kennedy: What's that?

Huxley: Wisdom and love, the two great virtues in Buddhism.

Lewis: Not just in Buddhism; universally, I think. In the Bible and in Greek philosophy too. Aristotle called them the intellectual virtues and the moral virtues.

Kennedy: Could you describe *karuna* more specifically?

Lewis: Gladly. *Karuna is* the kind of love that comes naturally to you when you are big and open of heart. It makes you humble.

Kennedy: Humble? I think of the humble person as small. You said *"big* of heart."

Lewis: Humble comes from *humus,* earth. Sages are earthy. They feel at home with you, and they make you feel at home with them. They are *with* you; their very being is a with-being: what Marcel calls *co-esse.* They are not thinking about themselves, but about you, caring about you. They are selfless not by being small but by being empty, open, commodious; they always have plenty of room in themselves for you and your needs.

Kennedy: I know exactly what you mean. We ordinary people try to have this quality, but we succeed only partially, and at times, and with a few people. They seem to be totally open at all times with everybody. It's a very rare and valuable quality, especially for a public leader.

(3)
Creativity
Lewis: If we agree about *karuna,* let's go on to the third quality of the sages: creativity. They can't be programmed, pinned down, predicted and controlled. They can't be classified in familiar categories.

Kennedy: Now that's the kind of admission I like to hear: no black-and-white categories.

Lewis: But they're not gray either. They're not a mixture, a muddle, a confusion; not a little wisdom and a little folly, a little good and a little evil. They're not gray, but colored. Another *dimension.*

Kennedy: Yes. That kind of creativity is in all the pioneers. That's why I'd call them progressives, or liberals.

Lewis: Haven't you just contradicted yourself? You agreed a minute ago that they couldn't be classified in familiar categories. And what categories are more familiar than those of liberal and conservative, left and right, radical and traditional. Talk about black-and-white thinking! Physician, heal thyself!

Kennedy: But surely to be creative is to be new rather than old, progressive rather than reactionary?

Lewis: I think you're a victim of your terminology. If you were a conservative, you'd use terms like *traditional vs. radical* rather than *progressive vs. reactionary.* Or *eternal vs. ephemeral* rather than *stagnant vs. dynamic.* But they say the same thing, only with different emotional overtones of approval or disapproval.

Kennedy: Let's look at the sages themselves rather than abstract terminology. The "liberal" classification will emerge naturally from the facts about their personality and history.

Lewis: Let's look, by all means. But I think we'll find that they're all unclassifiable as either Left or Right. Socrates, for instance, was executed by a conspiracy of Left and Right together: dogmatic establishmentarians and skeptical anti-establishmentarians, the "friends of the gods" and the new relativists, the Sophists. In fact, each group classified him as a friend of the other, and therefore their enemy. The same thing happened to Jesus, whose enemies included the dogmatic Pharisees and the skeptical Sadducees.

Are sages Right or Left?

Huxley: Shouldn't we add that in this case the dogmatists were the revisionists and the skeptics were the traditionalists?

Lewis: That's true, but let's not get bogged down in details.

Kennedy: I'd like to hear this "detail." It might help to overcome rigid classifications.

Lewis: All right. Briefly, the point Aldous stuck in was that the Pharisees believed in more (especially more *laws*) and the Sadducees less, because the Sadducees believed only the Pentateuch, the first five books of the Bible, as directly inspired by God. That's why they didn't believe in life after death: it's not mentioned until later, in Job and the Psalms and the prophets.

Kennedy: In any case, the point is that Jesus is like the other sages in not fitting into existing classifications of Right or Left?

Lewis: Yes.

Kennedy: It seems to me that on many issues they take the position of the Left.

Lewis: Do you think they take the position of the Right, or the Traditionalists, on some issues?

Kennedy: Well, yes. On some.

Lewis: And on some issues they take neither position?

Kennedy: Yes.

Lewis: And the most important issues are the ones they take the position of neither.

Kennedy: Yes, I'd have to agree with that. My study of great men of action has impressed me with their resourcefulness. They don't live by the book. They wouldn't have survived if they had. They adapt. They're creative.

Lewis: Good. And that's why they're so fascinating to listen to in dialog.

Kennedy: I think you have in mind creative *thinkers,* while I have in mind creative *actors,* men of action. But how are your creative thinkers fascinating in dialog?

The real question is the questioner. *Lewis:* You never know ahead of time what answer they're going to give. They don't give predigested pap, clichés. They give instead the answer the questioner really needs. They see that the real question is seldom the words. The real question is not the question but the questioner. They answer *him,* and their answer somehow turns the situation around so that *they* question *him.* He feels questioned, challenged, rather than the challenger. That's also why so many people feel threatened by the sages.

Kennedy: I can follow you all the way in this psychological description, and it seems to bear out *my* classification of Jesus rather than yours. He is not alone; he is one of the sages in all three ways. Like Solomon. Like a Zen master. Like Socrates.

Lewis: He is a typical sage in his sagacity. But not one of the other sages—not Moses, not Socrates, not Solomon, not Confucius, not Buddha—claimed to be God.

Kennedy: But as you pointed out before, he is not unique in that way either.

Lewis: No, but all the others who claim to be God are insane.

Kennedy: I don't really want to hold this position, but can you prove Jesus was *not* insane?

Lewis: Yes, as far as such things ever can be proved. And that will answer the second of your three questions. Having defined sagacity, we now define the divinity complex. And the juxtaposition of the two will answer your third question, how the two states are absolutely incompatible.

What is a divinity complex?

Kennedy: Go ahead.

Lewis: The psychological state of a person with a divinity complex is exactly the opposite of that of the sage in all three ways. First, the supposed "wisdom" of this "God" turns out to be mere platitudes that everyone knows and agrees with already. Nothing surprising, nothing original. He got them not from his own pioneering spiritual experience but second hand, verbally. He is a parrot.

(1) No wisdom

Kennedy: Right.

Lewis: Second, his ego is so small that it has no room in itself for you. He is hard, brittle and narrow. He clings to his illusion of divinity as "something to be grasped."

(2) No love

Kennedy: Isn't that a quotation from the New Testament?

Lewis: Yes. St. Paul describes Jesus in these terms: "Though he was in the form of God, he did not count equality with God a thing to be grasped, but emptied himself, taking the form of a servant, being born in the likeness of men." The person suffering from a divinity complex cannot empty himself because there is not much of a self there to empty. He is incapable of caring about you for the same reason he is incapable of insight into you: he is only into himself.

Kennedy: No *prajna* and no *karuna*.

Lewis: You get the feeling you're a mere walk-on in his play. However much he *tries* to be compassionate and humble (perhaps to imitate Jesus), it just doesn't come off.

Kennedy: And the creativity?

(3) No creativity   *Lewis:* Also not there. That's why he can't dialog. He never talks with you, just at you. All monolog. He's a monomaniac. And that doesn't make for a good listener. He's as predictable as a machine; he always gives the same answer to the same question no matter who asks it because he isn't really aware of you at all as a distinct individual. There is no other for him.

Kennedy: Ugh! What a small person!

Lewis: Yes, and no one ever said that about Jesus. "What a dangerous person!" perhaps, or even "What a blasphemous person!" but never "What a small person!"

Kennedy: So what is the logic of the argument now? We have agreed on our terms. Now prove the divinity of Jesus.

Classifying Christ   *Lewis:* Into which of the following three classes would you put him? Ordinary people, sages or pseudogods?

Kennedy: Sages, of course.

Lewis: No, for they do not claim to be God, and he does.

Kennedy: Hmmm. Suppose we try pseudogods?

Lewis: No, because they lack the wisdom, compassion and creativity that he has.

Kennedy: And not ordinary people, because . . .

Lewis: For both reasons. There is only one possibility left. How can it be avoided?

Kennedy: And that is?

Lewis: He is a sage, therefore to be trusted. And he claims to be God, therefore he is not just another human sage. *Aut deus aut homo malus.*

Kennedy: You sound like a combination between Socrates and Kierkegaard. The logical dialectic of Socrates' either-ors and the personal dialectic of Kierkegaard's either-or.

Lewis: Don't waffle. You're trying to avoid the argument by complimenting the arguer; an inverted *ad hominem.* What about the argument?

Kennedy: I can't honestly say I can refute the argument, nor can I honestly say I am convinced by it, no matter how unanswerable it seems to be.

Following an argument

Lewis: Would you agree that if an argument really is unanswerable, really and not just apparently is a successful argument, that it really proves its point?

Kennedy: Of course. That's what a successful argument *means.*

Lewis: And if it proves its point, its point is proved.

Kennedy: Of course.

Lewis: Proved to be what?

Kennedy: To be true, of course.

Lewis: And if a point is really proved to be true, then it is true, right?

Kennedy: Wait a minute. Something can be true without being proved to be true.

Lewis: Right. But can it be proved to be true without being true?

Kennedy: Of course not. All right, if it is really proved to be true, then it is true.

Have we really proved Christ's divinity?

Lewis: So the only question is whether we have here a good proof.

Kennedy: Right.

Lewis: Now let's review some elementary logic. What is a good proof? Is it not one in which no one of the many things that can possibly go wrong with a proof, or weaken it, does go wrong or weaken it?

Kennedy: Yes.

Lewis: Now the things that can go wrong with a proof depend on the kind of proof it is, inductive or deductive. The rules are different for different kinds of proofs.

Kennedy: Right.

Lewis: What kind of proof do we have here?

Kennedy: Deductive. It argues not from particular cases to a general principle but from a general principle to a particular case.

Lewis: Correct. Now what could possibly go wrong with a deductive proof?

Kennedy: Let's see. If I remember my logic, three things. It has something to do with each of the three "acts of the mind"— conception, judgment and reasoning, doesn't it?

Lewis: Yes. The logical products of those three acts are terms, propositions and arguments. And the three things that can go wrong are that the terms may be ambiguous, the propositions may be false and the argument may be fallacious.

Kennedy: I remember.

Lewis: Well, then, have we used a term ambiguously? Have we forgotten to define our terms? Did we disagree on any of the definitions?

Kennedy: No.

The terms are clear.

Lewis: Next: did we argue from false premises?

Kennedy: Review the basic argument for me again, please. What were the premises?

Lewis: The form of the argument we began with was the simple *aut deus aut homo malus, et non homo malus, ergo deus.* Either Jesus is God or a bad man. He is not a bad man. Therefore, he is God. Then we explained and expanded the argument by classifying people and defining sages. The second form of the argument was this: First premise: Jesus is a sage, and therefore trustable. Second premise: He claimed to be God.

Kennedy: Both those premises seem to be true.

The premises are true.

Lewis: Then the only question remaining is the logic of the argument. Is there any fallacy in arguing that if what trustable people say is true, and if this trustable person said he was God, then he was God?

Kennedy: The conclusion seems to follow if you accept the premises. But the first form of the argument seems weaker. I think I can still quarrel with that. The premise "either a bad man or God" is the black-and-white thinking I'm still suspicious of.

The logic is valid.

Lewis: That's where my fourfold classification comes in. It proves that either-or premise.

Kennedy: How?

Lewis: There are only four possibilities. He is either God, or a bad man (blasphemous or insane), or a good man (a mere sage), or an ordinary man. That's another way of stating the either-or premise, with four possibilities instead of two. And you can't classify Jesus in any one of the other three categories.

Kennedy: The conclusion seems to follow here too. Yet I don't want to be forced to admit that.

Lewis: Why not? If the argument really proves it, then it must be true. Don't you want to admit what's true?

Kennedy: Of course. But there must be something wrong with the argument.

Lewis: Why?

Kennedy: Well, I don't want to accept the conclusion.

Lewis: Do your wants determine the truth?

Kennedy: No, but I don't believe the conclusion is true.

Lewis: But if you cannot refute the argument, you must.

Being bullied by the truth

Kennedy: Must I, really? Why? I think I'm being bullied.

Lewis: By the truth, not by me. If you cannot refute the argument, you can mean only one thing by refusing the conclusion.

Kennedy: What?

Lewis: That you know it's true and still refuse to believe it; that you simply don't care about truth; that you don't *want* to know the truth. In short, that you are dishonest.

Kennedy: How dare you? I've not been dishonest with you. I've been quite candid.

Lewis: Yes, and I appreciate that. But you'd be dishonest with reality if you admitted that the argument proves the conclusion to be true and you still refuse to believe it. I don't think you *are* dishonest; that's why you will have to accept the conclusion.

Kennedy: Aldous, help!

Lewis: Go ahead, Aldous. But Jack, before he does, please ask yourself one question honestly.

Kennedy: What?

Lewis: Why are you so desperately looking for help?

Kennedy: Why, to win the argument, of course. I always hated losing.

Lewis: I thought we agreed at the beginning that this was to be an argument in which no one of us would win, only truth would win.

Kennedy: All right then, I still don't believe your conclusion is true.

Lewis: So you're looking for Aldous to help you find a way out of the argument because you don't want to believe its conclusion.

Kennedy: Right. I said that.

Lewis: Why? Why don't you want to believe it?

Kennedy: What do you mean? I just don't believe it, that's all.

The will to disbelieve

Lewis: Is it because you think it isn't true?

Kennedy: Of course.

Lewis: Or is it for some other reason?

Kennedy: What other reason? What are you suggesting?

Lewis: I am suggesting nothing. *Any* other reason would be a dishonest reason.

Kennedy: Why?

Only one honest reason for believing anything

Lewis: Why, because the only honest reason anyone ever has for believing anything is that they think it is *anything* true. Would it be honest to believe what you thought was false? And the only honest reason anyone ever has for disbelieving anything is that they think it is false. Would it be honest to disbelieve what you thought was true?

Kennedy: Well, no, of course not.

Lewis: No, not "of course." Too many "of courses." Many of your "of course" admissions would be strongly refused by most modern philosophers, and the millions of people they influence by osmosis. They would prefer to believe things for a hundred other reasons besides truth: relevance, practicality, advantage, comfort, interest, dynamism, challenge, power, novelty, happiness . . .

Truth or happiness first?

Kennedy: Do you think we can discount even happiness as a legitimate motive for belief? Can we come down so hard on the millions who believe a thing because it makes them happy?

Lewis: I'm not concerned with the millions here, only with you. Would you rather believe a lie that made you happy or the truth even if it made you unhappy?

Kennedy: I'm not sure. It's not an easy choice.

Lewis: I think it is, if you're honest. I think you would always rather believe the truth.

Kennedy: You mean I *should.* How could you tell what I *would* do? How do you know my motives?

Lewis: I think you *would.*

Kennedy: Prove that to me.

Lewis: I think I can. Look here: we're not fully in heaven yet, right? This is great fun, but it's certainly not the eternal bliss of the Beatific Vision. Now wouldn't you be much happier if it were?

Kennedy: Of course.

Lewis: And wouldn't you be much happier if you were convinced that it was heaven? Utterly, really convinced?

Kennedy: Of course. But I'm not.

Lewis: Why not? Why do you insist on your obstinate belief that you are not now in infinite joy?

Kennedy: What a silly question! I *know* I'm not.

Lewis: In other words, you know the truth about where you are.

Kennedy: Yes. *That* truth, anyway: that I'm not in heaven yet.

Lewis: Thus you prefer truth to happiness.

Kennedy: Why, it seems I do! But it's so natural. It seems we do that all the time. We know what we know.

Lewis: Until we are dishonest, until we turn from known or suspected truth because it threatens us, or turn to a known or suspected lie because it attracts us. Our mind is not impervious to suggestions from the will or emotions, you know.

Kennedy: I know. I'm not psychologically naive, you know. Frankly, I thought *you* were, the way you were arguing so rationalistically.

Lewis: You thought I was forgetting the psychological dimension of human argument.

Kennedy: Yes.

Lewis: The reason I couldn't do that is my own experience. I practiced just the sort of self-deceptive rationalization I've warned you about for many years. I hated the thought of a

God who literally barged into our world and our species, who interfered with our lives and our values and perhaps even our human nature. I hated it because I wanted to be on my own, to be my own boss, my own God. And I'm convinced that many people reject Christianity—traditional, biblical, orthodox Christianity, with its active, loving, interfering, demanding God—for that reason. Not because the evidence proves it's untrue, but because they don't *want* it to be true.

Kennedy: And you think that's what I'm doing?

Lewis: I don't know your heart. If the shoe fits, wear it. But doesn't honesty demand that you at least ask yourself the question seriously?

Kennedy: If the mind is as devious as you say, how can anyone know he's not practicing self-deception?

Honesty begins in the will. *Lewis:* That sounds like a very complicated and unanswerable question, but in fact the answer is shockingly simple. It's simply by wanting to.

Kennedy: Just wanting to?

Lewis: Yes. If the will moves the intellect, then that's where we must start. An honest will makes an honest mind. That's what Jesus was implying when they asked him how they could know whether his teaching was true, whether it really came from God or not, and he replied: "If your will were to do the will of my Father, you would know my teaching, that it comes from him."

Kennedy: Is that in the Bible?

Lewis: Yes. It's John 7:17.

Kennedy: It certainly simplifies the problem. Perhaps we design complexities to avoid uncomfortable simplicities. I shall have to think more deeply and honestly about all this. Frankly, you scare me, Lewis. You pull no punches. You must have made quite a few enemies when you were on earth.

Huxley: Since the argument has taken this personal and psychological turn, and since Jack seems about to go off somewhere to scrutinize his motives, could we return to the logic of the argument first, before he leaves? I'm not convinced that we've scrutinized the *argument* well enough yet to justify any of us scrutinizing his own soul for hidden motives in refusing the conclusion of such a so-called inescapable argument. I think there is an escape from your conclusion.

Lewis: And what is that?

Kennedy: Aldous, wait! Before you answer—I'm grateful to you for coming to my aid, but don't you think we should give Lewis here a rest? He's been at it with me for an hour now, and he's about to cross swords with you without any intermission. I don't know how you feel, Lewis, but I feel mentally exhausted.

Lewis: Oh, I'm not exhausted at all. In fact, I don't think you are mentally exhausted either, Jack. I don't think anyone ever is.

Kennedy: What? That's nonsense.

Lewis: I'm not *sure* it's true, but it's not nonsense. I suspect that it's only the body that gets tired, never the spirit. But since the spirit uses the body as its instrument, the tiredness of the instrument is often read mistakenly into the user. Be that as it may, I'm anxious to hear your so-called way out, Aldous. I suspect it may indeed be "way out," as they say nowadays. What is it?

Huxley: Actually, there are two—two very respectable and popular answers to your argument that are not "way out" at all. The first is simply to deny the premise that Jesus ever claimed to be divine. This lets us classify him with all those other human sages. Your argument won't work without the premise

II. Two escapes from the argument

that he claimed divinity, and you can't prove that premise.

(1)
Jesus never
claimed
divinity;
the texts
lie.

Lewis: Of course I can.

Huxley: How?

Lewis: As I can prove any historical statement: not by an abstract syllogism but by observation. Eyewitnesses saw and heard him. They told us about it, as they tell us about every event before our time: orally and in written form.

How
reliable
are the
Gospel
texts?

Huxley: So you rely on the textual evidence.

Lewis: Of course, just as you rely on the textual evidence for the teachings of Plato, or the deeds of Julius Caesar.

Huxley: And just how certain can a two-thousand-year-old text be?

Lewis: Do you doubt that Caesar was emperor, or that he conquered Gaul?

Huxley: No.

Lewis: Can you prove it?

Huxley: No. That's my whole point. It's merely a historical statement . . .

Lewis: But even so, even though it can't be proved as a mathematical statement can, still you do not doubt that Caesar conquered Gaul?

Huxley: Well . . . not really.

Lewis: Why not, if the texts don't *prove* it?

Huxley: They give evidence for it—the best evidence we have. And there seems no evidence against it, no reason to doubt the record.

Lewis: So you have two reasons for believing a historical event: textual evidence for it and no evidence against it.

Huxley: Yes.

Lewis: Well then, why don't you believe Jesus claimed divinity? There is plenty of textual evidence for it, and none against it.

Huxley: Because the New Testament texts are not like the accounts of Caesar's Gallic wars; they're myth, not history.

Lewis: How do you know that?

Huxley: If I read that Caesar was virgin born, or rose from the dead, I'd think Caesar's story was myth too.

Are the Gospels myth or history?

Lewis: So you think the Gospels are myth only because they contain miracle stories.

Huxley: I suppose so.

Lewis: I think you are arguing in a circle.

Huxley: How? I don't see that at all.

Lewis: You think Jesus never really claimed divinity, right?

Huxley: Right.

Lewis: And that he was not really born of a virgin, or literally rose from the dead, right?

Huxley: Right.

Lewis: And your justification for doubting that these things really happened is that the evidence is not conclusive, right?

Huxley: Right. The only evidence is the claim of the texts. It's not that Jesus claimed to be divine, but that the texts claim that Jesus claimed to be divine. I think I'd trust what Jesus said, but I don't necessarily trust all the texts say.

Lewis: So you doubt Jesus claimed divinity because you doubt the texts.

Huxley: Yes.

Lewis: But the reason you doubt the texts is because you think they're only myth, not history, right?

Huxley: Right.

The circular argument of the demythologizers

Lewis: And the reason you think they're myth and not history is because they contain miracle stories like a God becoming a man and claiming divinity.

Huxley: Oh, oh. I see. That does look like a circular argument.

Lewis: Certainly. You doubt the miracle because you doubt the text, and you doubt the text because you doubt the miracle it describes.

Huxley: But surely it is correct to classify a text as myth when it is full of miracle stories instead of sober history.

Lewis: Only if you assume a prior philosophical belief that miracles can't happen. You approach the texts with that philosophy in mind. You don't decide whether a text is myth or history on a purely textual basis, a neutral and scientific basis, as you claim. If your philosophy allowed you to believe in miracles, you would accept the biblical accounts of miracles as readily as you accept secular accounts of wars. The biblical texts are at least as well established as any secular ones.

Huxley: What do you mean by that?

Lewis: That many undoubted and universally accepted events in secular history have far less textual evidence than the events in the Gospels. They are written later, longer after the event; and there are fewer copies of them for cross-checking. If it didn't contain anything miraculous, biblical history would be accepted as certainly as secular history.

Huxley: But Lewis, surely you as a literary man are aware of the advances in form criticism. The issue is not as simple as you make it sound. Hermeneutics is no easy thing.

Kennedy: Herman who?

Huxley: Hermeneutics. The science of interpretation, especially of texts and of literary forms, such as the difference between the literary form of myth and that of history. Form criticism has simply demolished the naive belief that the Bible is historically accurate.

Lewis: It has done no such thing. When you properly use it, it does not reduce history to myth, nor myth to history. It tells us to read poetry as poetry and prose as prose, symbolism as symbolism and eyewitness descriptions as eyewitness descriptions. And the Gospels are full of eyewitness descriptions.

Huxley: Then why are most form critics demythologizers?

Lewis: Because of their philosophy, not their literary evidence. Most of them simply assume that miracles do not happen and then read all miracle texts as myth, whether they have the literary form of myth or not. That's simply bad form criticism; it reads the form not in literary but in philosophical terms.

Huxley: And who is responsible for such a foolish error?

Lewis: The most famous is a certain rude, elf-built man . . .

Huxley: Rudolf Bultmann? Surely "demythologizing" goes back much further than that.

Lewis: Indeed it does: to the eighteenth century, and even the seventeenth with Spinoza. But Bultmann made demythologizing a household word.

Huxley: In fact, it goes back to the Gnostics of the first few centuries of the Christian era.

The origin of demythologizing: Gnosticism

Lewis: I had heard you called a modern Gnostic. You accept the classification, then?

Huxley: Yes.

Lewis: The Manichees were Gnostics of a sort, weren't they?

Huxley: Of a sort.

Lewis: They had a special, symbolic or mystical interpretation of Scripture, didn't they, like the Gnostics?

Huxley: Yes.

Lewis: It seems to me St. Augustine's argument against them still stands up.

Huxley: What argument is that?

Lewis: It's in the *Confessions,* book 5, chapter 11. A certain Elpidius had refuted them from Scripture, and the Manichees' answer, Augustine says, "seemed to me feeble—indeed they preferred not to give it in public but only among ourselves in private (Augustine was a Manichee)—the answer being that the Scriptures of the New Testament had been corrupted."

Huxley: What's so "feeble" about that answer?

Lewis: Augustine goes on to say, "yet the Manicheans made no effort to produce uncorrupted copies."

Huxley: Ah, but there *are* early Gnostic texts, like the Gospel of St. Thomas.

Gnostic texts vs. New Testament texts

Lewis: Which were consistently declared noncanonical by the church, and which consistently manifested the literary style of myth, with its arbitrarily scattered stories of magic, rather than the sober eyewitness narrative style of the Gospels. Those two features clearly distinguish the Gnostic materials from the orthodox ones.

Huxley: Let's analyze your two features one by one. For the first charge to stand up, you have to take the Catholic position rather than the Protestant one on the relation between the Scriptures and the church. Yet you are not a Catholic.

Lewis: Why must I take the Catholic line?

Huxley: Do you believe in the principle of causality?

Lewis: Of course. I used it with Jack a few minutes ago.

Huxley: So the effect cannot be greater than its cause?

Lewis: No.

Huxley: Then how can a fallible church infallibly determine the canon of the infallible Scriptures?

Lewis: That's an old argument, but I'd rather not get into it right now if you don't mind. As I said before, I've studiously avoided all disputes between different churches in my writings in order to concentrate on "mere Christianity." I just feel on much firmer ground talking about the second criterion, the literary one. That's my field, after all.

Huxley: I'll grant you your own playing field. What are the literary criteria for rejecting the Gnostic materials and accepting the traditional ones?

Lewis: The whole flavor is different, the whole atmosphere.

Huxley: How? Legends sprang up around the founders of every religion: Buddha, Muhammad, Lao-Tzu. Why couldn't the accounts of Jesus rising from the dead be later additions just as the accounts of Muhammad riding his horse to the moon, or Buddha being showered with flower petals from the gods?

Lewis: First of all, there is a substantive reason; second, one of style. Miracles have no place in Islam or Buddhism. Muhammad claimed that Allah dictated the Qur'an word for word, and that was to have been the *only* miracle in Islam. Buddha taught that the separate reality of the material world was an illusion; working miracles in that world would foster the illusion, not dispel it. But the *essential* claim of Jesus is miraculous; drop the miraculous from Christianity and you get a wholly different religion. That's not true of Islam or Buddhism.

Christianity essentially miraculous

Huxley: How do you get a different religion?

Lewis: You get Christianity minus the incarnation, redemption and the resurrection. Christianity is the good *news*. Without those events, it's no news at all.

Huxley: It's news to meet a man like Jesus. He's a new kind of man.

Lewis: How is he new?

Huxley: Your Gospels themselves put it quite simply and adequately: "He went about doing good."

Lewis: But what good did he do? Did he visit prisoners? Did he clothe the naked? Did he clean up local politics? No. He did *miracles*. Eliminate them and there's not much left that he did.

Huxley: Hmmm. I never thought of it that way. But let's get on to your second distinction, the one of style. You said the whole flavor of the Gospels was different from legends. You haven't proved that to me yet. You're going against the whole stream of textual scholarship in the twentieth century, you know.

Lewis: I know. I never had my nose to the tail of the twentieth century. And I know something about texts too, you know, especially about myths. My whole literary life and love is woven around them. The Gospels simply don't fit their literary mold.

Huxley: Why not?

Lewis: The realistic details, for one thing.

Huxley: Which?

Lewis: Little things, like Jesus writing in the sand when they brought the accused adultress to him for judgment. Just the sort of thing an eyewitness would have thrown in, without understanding it any more than we do, but *not* the sort of thing a maker of legends would invent. For another thing, names and dates to pin the story down in history. Legends are vague at best about them. Also, psychological asides, hundreds of little insights into character that legends simply do not have— they don't try to. Their literary form has no room for that dimension.

Huxley: But even granted these differences, what do they prove?

Lewis: That if the Gospels are not eyewitness accounts, then they are a type of fantasy that has absolutely no parallel in all of literature. That some Galilean peasants—fishermen and tax collectors—invented not only the world's most gigantic and successful hoax but a totally unique form of literature, the realistic fantasy.

The unique literary form of the Gospels

Huxley: Unlikely, if I accept your analysis, but still possible. At this point the argument is inconclusive.

Lewis: Ah, but do you see what the inconclusiveness means logically?

Huxley: What?

Lewis: This is your objection we are investigating, not my original argument.

Huxley: Yes. I'm attacking a premise you need for your argument, namely, that Jesus really claimed divinity.

Lewis: And since your attack is inconclusive, my argument still stands.

Huxley: Not against my second objection, it doesn't. I think there are still many things to be said about this first objection, but rather than beat an inconclusive horse, I'd like to get on to a simple, strong and clear objection that can admit the validity of your texts and still escape your *aut deus* argument.

Lewis: Object away.

The second escape: *All are divine like Jesus.*

Huxley: The second objection admits that Jesus claimed divinity but understands that claim in the same way we should understand the similar claim of thousands of Hindu and Buddhist mystics. They also claim divinity *and are not insane,* so Jesus is not the only one who fits your fourth category. Nearly every enlightened mystic says the same thing. Jesus uses a personal metaphor; he calls God his Father. Others use different metaphors: we are drops in the divine ocean, sparks from the divine fire, thoughts in the divine mind, cells in the divine body, characters in the divine drama. It comes to the same thing. Jesus is a teacher of the "perennial philosophy" in Hebrew; the guru to the Jews.

Lewis: "The perennial philosophy"—that's the title of your anthology of the writings of the mystics, isn't it?

Huxley: Yes. It was my favorite book.

Lewis: You mean *Brave New World* wasn't your favorite?

Huxley: No, only my readers' favorite, just as *The Screwtape Letters* was your readers' favorite, but I'll bet it wasn't yours. Was it?

Lewis: No. I had to put my imagination in hell to write letters from a devil. It seems you did something a little similar in *Brave New World* in imagining the hell of modernity in its apotheosis.

Huxley: Yes. And not far away, if you follow *Brave New World Revisited.* But back to the argument: "the perennial philosophy" is that of every great sage and spiritual master, including Jesus of Nazareth. He is great, but he is not unique.

Pantheism *Lewis:* You've stated a very important and very widely held position, I think. Whether it is true or not still remains to be seen. Let's find out by first defining our terms. This "perennial philosophy" is basically pantheism, is it not?

Huxley: No, I don't like that word.

Lewis: I didn't ask that. I asked whether "the perennial philosophy" was pantheism or not.

Huxley: Not if you mean it in the Western sense.

Lewis: What is "the Western sense"?

Huxley: You begin with the Western notion of God, of *theos,* and then you say that all, pan, is that *theos.*

Lewis: And by the Western notion of God you mean . . . ?

Huxley: A personal Creator distinct from his creation.

Lewis: That is the Western notion of God.

Huxley: Yes. And to say that the God who is distinct from all things is all things, is simply nonsense.

Lewis: A self-contradiction.

Huxley: Yet it contains a kernel of truth in a misshapen nut of words.

Lewis: And that truth is . . .

Huxley: That all is one.

Lewis: Monism.

Huxley: You may use that label as long as you don't interpret it as a static "block of stuff." The One is spirit, dynamism, life, consciousness.

Lewis: I'm familiar with the idea. In fact, I nearly believed it myself once.

Huxley: Oh? When was that?

Lewis: I described it in my autobiography, *Surprised by Joy.* When I stopped being an atheist and started investigating the claims of the world's great religions, I came to the conclusion that Hinduism and Christianity were ultimately the only two options.

Huxley: Perceptive of you. But they're not two. They're one. There's your mistake: another example of your either-or, black-and-white thinking. You can't see that all religions are one at their mystical core, just as all reality is one at its mystical core. Which is inevitable, since religion is about reality.

Lewis: I agree that religion is about reality. Whether reality is one is a great question of philosophy, and not easily settled. But whether all religions are one is a question of observation, and it is easily settled: just look at their teachings. They're *not* the same. They teach contradictory things.

Esoteric vs. exoteric religion

Huxley: They seem to. But that's only on the surface level, not at their core. Perhaps you've read Fritjof Schuon's *The Transcendent Unity of Religions?* Alan Watts made the same point in a more popular and lively style: that there are two levels or dimensions in religion—the exoteric and the esoteric, the outer and the inner, the public and the private, the revealed and the hidden. The outer shell of a religion is its creed, code and cult; its words, works and worship. But the kernel, the inner essence, is the experience of oneness.

Lewis: It seems to me you are saying that Christianity and Buddhism are very much alike, especially Buddhism.

Huxley: You plagiarized that from Chesterton!

Lewis: Yes, I did. I'm glad you have read him.

Huxley: What does it mean?

Lewis: That you're using Oriental categories to interpret Christianity; you're Orientalizing Christianity, synthesizing by annexation-spiritual imperialism.

Huxley: Why do you say that?

Lewis: Because the esoteric-exoteric distinction is itself an esoteric, not an exoteric doctrine. It applies to esoteric Eastern religions but not to exoteric Western religions. Judaism, Christianity and Islam are public, open, democratic religions, religions of a Book, open for all to read, not religions of hidden experiences known only to the initiated mystics. They are religions of history and of the deeds and words of God in history. Christianity is ultimately the Word of God in history. All public facts, not private mysticism.

Huxley: You're probably one of those suspicious fellows who think mysticism begins in mist, centers in "I" and ends in schism.

Lewis: Actually, I had a different quip up my sleeve: Ronald Knox's remark about "comparative religion."

Huxley: What's that?

Lewis: That it makes you comparatively religious.

Huxley: So you're not sympathetic to ecumenism?

Lewis: Not when it involves fuzzy thinking and ignoring contradictions.

Huxley: Contradictions appear only on the outer level, the exoteric. If you would penetrate to the inner core, you would find all contradictions resolved in The One. But you ignore that deepest level.

Lewis: In Christianity the deepest level came out in public: "In him all the fullness of God was pleased to dwell." I'm not ignoring esoteric Christianity; how could I ignore something that doesn't exist? It's your invention.

Huxley: It's certainly in the mystics, and there are plenty of Christian mystics, you know.

Lewis: Our orthodox mystics, like Bernard of Clairvaux or John of the Cross, only experience the truths of the public dogmas, the exoteric revelation. The heretical or heterodox mystics, like Meister Eckhart, seem to contradict the dogmas, and they are the only ones you can enlist on the side of "the perennial philosophy" of monism. So Christianity does not involve esoteric mysticism, only exoteric mysticism.

Huxley: You may label Eckhart a heretic, but surely you won't label Jesus one. Yet he taught "the perennial philosophy" too, once you peel away the cultural baggage.

Lewis: The cultural baggage?

Huxley: Excuse the mixed metaphor. Jesus translated the perennial philosophy into terms limited by Jewish culture.

Jesus, the guru to the Jews?

Lewis: So Jesus was the guru to the Jews, as Lao-Tzu was the guru to the Chinese?

Huxley: Yes. He translated the universal truth into Semitic terms, and the world has gotten hung up on the terms and missed the truth.

Lewis: And the truth is monism?

Huxley: Yes. And Jesus is a guru, not a God.

Lewis: I'm glad you put it so simply and strongly.

Huxley: Why?

Lewis: Because now I can refute it simply and strongly.

Huxley: Thanks for the left-handed compliment!

Lewis: Seriously, foolish and confused errors need tedious and confusing refutations, but it takes a clear and strong mind to utter something so clearly refutable.

Huxley: Then let's hear this "clear refutation," please. I'm sure the perennial philosophy is not going to collapse like a house of cards under the logic-chopping of an Oxford don! The greatest minds in the world know it to be true by experience.

Lewis: They may have experienced the mystic unity, but they can't possibly have experienced your contention that Jesus taught it.

Huxley: Why not?

Lewis: Why, because they weren't around to hear him, of course.

Huxley: That's silly. Of course not. How could they?

Lewis: But all the texts, all the eyewitness accounts of Jesus, all the data show the opposite: that he taught not pantheism but theism; not that God was everything but that God was the Creator of everything; not that we are all innately divine, but that we must become divine; not that we are all part of perfect divinity but that we are in sin and need a Savior . . .

Huxley: Whoa, there! Too much at once. Let's stop and sort out these apparent differences.

Lewis: Yes, let's. And when we see them, we shall see the clear refutation of your idea that Jesus is just the guru to the Jews, that he meant to preach the same thing as Lao-Tzu and Buddha. Because if he did, then he was the most spectacularly unsuccessful and misleading teacher in all of human history.

Huxley: What? Why?

Lewis: Because he consistently fostered a number of illusions, from your monist viewpoint, and led all his followers down the wrong path for centuries, until finally two thousand years later some scholars like you finally come along and figure out that he really meant exactly the opposite of what he said.

Huxley: Ridiculous!

Lewis: My point exactly.

Huxley: Let's get to specifics. What are these "illusions," these "mistakes" that Jesus taught?

Lewis: "Mistakes" from *your* point of view, not mine. Contradictions to the perennial philosophy of the gurus.

Huxley: Well, what are they?

Lewis: There are at least six of them.

Six crucial differences between Jesus and the gurus

Huxley: Oh, oh. If these six points are as central as you say, we may need six more dialogs. Could you make your points as short and sweet as possible?

Lewis: Short, yes. Sweet is in the tongue of the taster. But I'll try to make them as short and simple as possible, at the risk of radically oversimplifying.

Huxley: Oversimplify away.

Lewis: I said "the *risk* of oversimplifying"; I'll try to avoid it.

Huxley: Proceed.

(1) God as personal

Lewis: First, Jesus clearly believed and taught that God is personal, not impersonal. He prayed to his Father. He loved to pray from the Psalms, even on the cross; remember "My God, My God, why hast thou forsaken me?"

Huxley: That was only his local limitation, his cultural expression, his Jewishness as distinct from his universality. The core is universal, the outer linguistic shell is particular.

Lewis: But in Judaism—certainly the Judaism of Jesus' time, at any rate—the personality of God and the will of God are precisely the inner core, *not* the outer shell.

Huxley: Prove it.

Lewis: Who is the greatest prophet, according to the Jews?

Huxley: Moses.

Lewis: Right. Now what makes a prophet great?

Huxley: The question is too broad to answer. There are dozens of ways of being great.

Lewis: Right again. I mean great *as a prophet.* To find out why Moses is the greatest prophet, we must know what a great prophet is, and to find out what a great prophet is, we must find out what a prophet is.

Huxley: Must we really do all that?

Lewis: If we want to be sure, yes. I'll make it quick and painless. A prophet is a mouth.

Huxley: A mouth?

Lewis: Yes. God's mouthpiece. The human instrument through which God reveals himself.

Huxley: So a great prophet is a great mouth.

Lewis: Yes, one through whom God reveals more of himself. So Moses is the greatest prophet for the Jews because God revealed more of himself through Moses than through anyone else. All right so far?

Huxley: Yes. But what did God reveal through Moses and no one else?

Lewis: His name.

Huxley: He has many names.

Lewis: No, we *give* him many names. Only once did he tell us his own name, not our name for him but his name for himself. And he told that to Moses.

Huxley: You mean I AM?

Lewis: Yes.

Huxley: We've been through that before, with Jack here.

Lewis: But my point here is that this is the name for a person, whether human or divine, earthly or unearthly. I-ness, egohood (not egotism)—the nature of ultimate reality for a Jew and for Jesus. Now what is this ego according to your perennial philosophy?

Huxley: It is the ultimate illusion, the ultimate block to Enlightenment.

Ego, the ultimate reality or the ultimate illusion?

Lewis: Precisely. Therefore Jesus taught exactly the opposite of what the gurus teach on the most ultimate question of all, the nature of God, the nature of ultimate reality.

Huxley: To call God ego is the ultimate anthropomorphism. The human reality projected out onto the divine. How can you be so grasping toward your little ego that you don't see that? You're making God in your own image.

Lewis: Or vice versa. The biblical explanation of the divine name equally fits the facts: that God made us in his image.

Huxley: What are "the facts" here?

Lewis: Two. One, that we experience ourselves as I, as self-conscious persons, whether that experience is true or illusory. Two, that the Jews, who claim to be God's chosen people, claim to have been told by God himself through his greatest prophet, Moses, that his own name is I AM—whether that claim is true or false. Those are the facts. Two opposite hypotheses have been offered to explain those facts: first, my biblical point of view, which says that God created us in his own image, that we are I's because he is I; and second, your pantheistic point of view which says that we created God in our own image and that both the human and the divine egos are illusory.

Huxley: Precisely. And now let me show you why my hypothesis is infinitely superior.

Lewis: But that would take another whole dialog. The point of this one is about Jesus, and I took this rather long road back to the burning bush only to prove one point: that right or wrong, Jesus taught the opposite theology from yours and your gurus'.

Huxley: I have a hypothesis that explains that too. He could not have confined himself to such illusion and anthropomorphism. The Jews simply misunderstood him, both his disciples and his enemies. Mysticism is not an easy philosophy to understand or accept, you know, and it would be the most natural thing in the world for them to misinterpret him, to translate his radically different teaching into terms more comfortable and familiar to them.

Lewis: But there is absolutely no evidence of that, in the scriptural records, in tradition, in history. In fact, the terms in which his teaching is recorded in the New Testament are already as radical and uncomfortable, especially to a Jew, as anything could possibly be.

Huxley: It is still quite possible that he taught the perennial philosophy in an esoteric way, and only his exoteric teaching was recorded.

Lewis: But there is simply no textual evidence at all of such an esoteric teaching. There are a lot of things his disciples didn't understand at first, but they all became clear later— like his death and resurrection and fulfillment of Old Testament prophecies—and none of them are esoteric. They're all public.

Huxley: We are free to draw opposite conclusions, as we do, from the same data.

Lewis: From what data do you draw your esoteric conclusion? You ignore all the data we do have, Scripture and tradition.

Huxley: Orthodox tradition, yes. But there are the Gnostics too, remember. *They* were esoteric Christians.

Lewis: They were esoteric, but they were not Christians. They were heretics.

Huxley: Only judged by orthodox standards. By Gnostic standards, orthodox Christianity is a heresy. By what right do you judge Gnosticism by orthodox standards rather than orthodoxy by Gnostic standards?

Lewis: We're talking about Jesus. Jesus was a Jew. The Gnostics were non-Jewish in their philosophy on all six of the issues we're talking about.

Huxley: Correct. And early Christianity made the mistake of reverting to Judaism.

Lewis: Reverting from what?

Huxley: Jesus' revolutionary Gnostic teaching, which his Jewish disciples misunderstood.

Lewis: And where did he get this teaching? He was born and brought up in Judaism, not in India or Egypt or Persia. How utterly unhistorical to imagine a deracinated Jesus in the teeth of all the textual evidence! Why lift Jesus from his context in history?

Huxley: Not *all* the textual evidence, if you please . . .

Kennedy: Excuse me for interrupting, but I'd like to hear the rest of Lewis's six points, and if we start poking around in the mare's nest of textual evidence we're going to get off the track for a long time.

Lewis: I agree, especially since these six points are my answer to Huxley's imaginary Gnostic Jesus and mystical Jesus and Orientalized Jesus. They show the Jewishness of Jesus.

Huxley: They may show the Jewishness of the Jesus of the orthodox texts, but not the historical Jesus, unless you assume an identity between the two; that is, unless you assume the orthodox texts are reliable.

Kennedy: And that's the mare's nest. Lewis has at least cast doubts on my doubts with his textual arguments a while back; I think that's all we can expect from one conversation. Let's get on with the other five points.

Huxley: All right, especially since I find even in the orthodox texts much evidence for Jesus as guru rather than God, and Lewis doesn't. So we can still argue from them. What is your second issue on which Jesus taught the opposite thing from the gurus, Lewis?

Lewis: God as Creator. For Jews, God is absolutely distinct from his creation. No other religion or philosophy in the entire history of the world ever came up with the thought that God created the world out of nothing.

(2) God as Creator

Huxley: Islam as well as Christianity . . .

Lewis: Simply follow Judaism on this point.

Huxley: Yes, but *all* the religions of the world picture God or the gods as some sort of creator or originator of the world. Does the technical point of creation out of nothing rather than out of something make such a crucial difference to your picture of God?

Lewis: It makes a crucial difference to your picture of the *world.* In the three Western religions that accept the Genesis account, the world is *not* God *and* not an illusion. In Eastern religions, the world is either God or an illusion, either part of God's mind or body, or *maya,* a trick.

Huxley: Again I ask, why is this point crucial?

Lewis: Because it is not just "this point." It characterizes the whole religion, this real distinction between Creator and creature, this separate reality of creatures.

Huxley: How?

Lewis: One feature of everything in the created world, mind as well as matter, is time.

Huxley: Yes.

Is time real?

Lewis: Now is time real or not?

Huxley: Ultimately, no. Not according to the mystics.

Lewis: But if God created the world, time is real. That's why Christianity, like Judaism, takes history seriously. It is a historical religion, a story, an eyewitness account of deeds and words in the world. Christianity is "the gospel," the good *news.* But in Eastern religions, the only gospel is that time is an illusion, that there is no news.

Huxley: No news is good news.

Lewis: Touché. An apt way to put it. But surely you see the extreme difference.

Huxley: The gurus teach detachment from the world-illusion, from time and space and matter and the body. But Christianity is pretty strong on detachment too, you know.

Lewis: From greed and egotism and selfishness, yes. But not from the world itself.

Huxley: What about the advice to "love not the world"? That's John the Evangelist. And what about "the world, the flesh and the devil" as the three great enemies?

Lewis: If you look up the Greek, you'll find that the word for "world" is *aion:* eon, era. It's a time word, not a space word. It means: Love not the old order. Christ has come and changed history. Love the new reality, the Body of Christ in history, not the old reality, the fallen and unredeemed world order.

Huxley: But doesn't Christianity hope for liberation *from* the world into paradise?

Lewis: No. Not paradise. Heaven.

Huxley: What's the difference?

Lewis: Paradise is Eden. That's behind us. Heaven is ahead. Look at the different imagery Eastern and Western religions use. Eastern religions are constantly picturing Enlightenment as a *return*—to the "uncarved virgin block," to the innocence and simplicity and purity of childhood . . .

Nostalgia vs. hope

Huxley: Seems to me there was a guru named Jesus who said the same thing: "Unless you turn and become like little children, you will never enter the kingdom of heaven."

Lewis: "*Become* like little children," yes; not "*remain* little children."

Huxley: What's the difference?

Lewis: There's progress, change, growth, maturing, the forward direction. For another thing, we're to become as little children only in some ways, not all.

Huxley: Which ways?

Lewis: Humility and trust.

Huxley: How do you know that's what he meant?

Lewis: That seems to be what he's talking about in the context, and in the broader context of his life and teachings in general. He's constantly appealing to hope, and making promises. He's very future-oriented.

Huxley: The modern illusion of progress.

Lewis: No, not progress; hope. Not *automatic* progress, and not *human* progress, but hope in God's promises. Count the promises in the Bible sometime; there are over three hundred of them, three hundred distinct promises.

Huxley: But there is also nostalgia . . . Eden . . . the biblical version of the universal myth of Paradise Lost.

Lewis: But in the biblical version, God blocks this natural nostalgia. After the Fall, he sends a seraphim with a flaming sword to bar the east gate of Eden so that Adam and Eve can't get back into Paradise. They have to seek God now "East of Eden," through time and history and the world and struggle and suffering and death.

Huxley: Why *"East* of Eden"?

Lewis: That's where the rising sun comes from.

Huxley: The Rising Son? Christ?

Lewis: A providential coincidence, maybe; at least, a profound pun. The point is, Christians and Jews look to history, to the future, for their Savior, their Messiah.

Huxley: A foolish mistake. They should look to eternity.

Lewis: But the point is that they *do* look to history, or to the eternal God's deeds and words in history. That's what the whole Bible is about. And that's very different from Eastern religions. My only point here is not that Jews and Christians are right (though of course I believe they are), just that they're different from the gurus.

Huxley: Only because they misunderstood the profoundest level of the teaching of their own guru.

Lewis: There you go again, inventing an Eastern esoteric teaching that simply isn't there!

Huxley: It's not so simple, you know. The texts will often bear a profoundly esoteric interpretation. Like "The kingdom of God is within you."

Lewis: The Greek there could equally well mean "is *among* you," or "in the midst of you."

Huxley: We must argue about texts some other day. Let's get on with the third difference.

Lewis: Right. The pantheist's God is beyond all duality, correct? **(3) God as knowable**

Huxley: Correct.

Lewis: Therefore beyond the duality of knower and known, mind and its contents, subject and object of thought, correct?

Huxley: Correct. Nondualistic consciousness is Enlightenment.

Lewis: And that is why God is unknowable, correct?

Huxley: As an object, yes.

Lewis: God is not an object, therefore not an object of thought.

Huxley: Yes. Therefore not knowable.

Lewis: But for Jews and Christians, God is knowable.

Huxley: What? The Infinite Being knowable by finite human minds? What foolishness!

Lewis: Not knowable in his essential nature, and not knowable naturally. But he makes himself knowable in his acts. He reveals himself in visible deeds and written words.

Huxley: Do you really believe that God literally spoke to men? That his hand wrote the Ten Commandments on Moses' stone tablets?

Lewis: The Bible says he did.

Huxley: But surely you are not so naive as that, Lewis. After all, you're a literary scholar.

Lewis: So? I've found scholars to be at least as naive as non-scholars, though about different things.

Huxley: Don't you honestly think it much more likely that the Jews simply read God *into* their history? That looking back on some wonderful event like the Exodus from Egypt, they interpreted it religiously and then wrote up this interpretation in mythic symbols like a miraculous parting of the Red Sea?

Lewis: No, I honestly don't.

Huxley: Why not? For reasons of faith only?

Lewis: No, for literary reasons too.

Huxley: Could you give me one?

Lewis: I'll give you two. First of all, a literary critic should ask of a story first of all what the whole story *is about,* and interpret particular events in the context of the whole story. And the story in the Bible is about God's search for man . . .

Huxley: You mean man's search for God.

**Man's
search
for God
vs. God's
search for
man**

Lewis: No. From the biblical point of view, speaking about man's search for God is like speaking about the mouse's search for the cat.

Huxley: You wrote that somewhere.

Lewis: Yes. I'm allowed to plagiarize myself. The point is that the God of the Bible invades man's world of time rather than man mystically invading God's eternity. Man searches for God in God's home, eternity, but God searches for man in man's home, time. And that's the God of the Bible, the Hound of Heaven, the divine lover, the Father looking for his prodigal son, the shepherd for his lost sheep. God takes the initiative. God always takes the initiative, from the act of creation on. The supreme example is the incarnation, the supreme example of taking history and time and the created world seriously. Instead of the passive Eastern God receiving man's search, man's spiritual efforts, Jesus is himself the active Western God barging into man's world physically.

Huxley: Physically? Come now, that's a rather crude interpretation of the incarnation, isn't it?

Lewis: Was he born out of a woman's body, or not?

Huxley: Ah, but we must penetrate the deeper meaning of these mythic symbols.

Lewis: The events of the gospel are not merely symbols. They're an account of what people saw and heard and did. And that brings me to my second literary reason for not buying your mythic interpretation. As I pointed out before, the literary form of the Gospels is strikingly different from myth. You can see myth in Homer, in Hesiod, in the *Eddas,* in the *Nibelungenlied* . . .

Huxley: And in the New Testament.

Lewis: Actually, you're right. There is one book in the New Testament written in mythic, symbolic form: the book of Revelation. And you can see the difference between gospel history and myth by comparing the Gospels with Revelation. The Gospels are sober eyewitness accounts of present events on earth; Revelation is poetic symbolism, dream imagery, things nobody sees in the outside world.

Huxley: Here we go into the textual issues again. Let's finish our six points first. Perhaps we'll come back to the issue of demythologizing again before we're through.

Lewis: Right. The fourth difference between the theology of Jesus and that of the gurus is that the god of the gurus is beyond all dualism, therefore also beyond the dualism of good and evil, beyond morality.

(4) God as good, not "beyond good and evil"

Huxley: That's right; and that follows from ultimate oneness just as the previous point did, the fact that man does not know God as an object, with dualistic subject-object *knowledge.* For the same reason, there is no dualistic *will.*

Lewis: But the God of Jesus is definitely good, not evil; righteous, not unrighteous; loving, not hating or indifferent. "God is light and in him is no darkness at all."

Huxley: Another profound exoteric illusion, and one that has done the world untold psychological harm.

Lewis: Oh? How?

Huxley: By making us try to be like this God, perfectly good with no evil, light without darkness. Impossible for us, and thus the cause of endless frustration and guilt.

Morality as a *koan*

Lewis: That's the Bad News at the back of the Good News, the diagnosis of the disease which is presupposed by the Gospel's prognosis of healing. In fact, morality works like a *koan* in Zen, one of those unsolvable puzzles that aren't *meant* to be solved by our own efforts, but to open us up for something greater.

Huxley: Something greater than morality?

Lewis: Certainly. Mount Sinai isn't in the Promised Land. But the road to it runs past the mountain.

Huxley: I don't see the point of your symbolism.

Lewis: The Law, which was given at Mount Sinai, is an indispensable preliminary to salvation. It's like a mirror which shows us our warts. But it can't remove them.

Huxley: That puts us in a pretty kettle of fish.

Lewis: Exactly. And we are saved from it by the divine fisherman.

Huxley: It seems to me that you have devised a complicated salvation myth to solve a problem that never should have been a problem in the first place. It should have been dissolved, not solved.

Lewis: Morality, you mean?

Huxley: Yes, morality. The God who is beyond good and evil is not a God who tortures us with morality. He fits our own doubleness. He includes and transcends both good and evil just as we do.

Lewis: Which God seems to be the anthropomorphic projection of ourselves now?

Huxley: I still say your God, because he is a projection of what you desire to be: good without evil.

Lewis: No, my desire to be good is a response to what God has revealed: that he is perfectly good and that his will is for us to be perfectly good.

Huxley: Where is that in Judaism?

Lewis: "You shall be holy; for I the LORD your God am holy."

Huxley: Where is it in Christianity?

Lewis: "Be ye perfect even as your Father in Heaven is perfect."

Huxley: Well, then the result must be tremendous frustration.

Lewis: No, hope. Remember, the Bible is full of promises.

Huxley: And meanwhile, while you're waiting, you worry your head off with guilt.

Lewis: No, the guilt is taken care of on Calvary, and there's no need to worry anymore. Jesus is constantly assuring his disciples of that. Look at all the "fear nots."

Huxley: Look here, does your God care about morality or not?

Lewis: He does.

Huxley: And are you supposed to care about morality too?

Lewis: Yes.

Huxley: And yet your God keeps telling you not to worry.

Lewis: That's right.

Huxley: Well, how can you care without worrying?

How to   *Lewis:* "Teach us to care and not to care," as Eliot put it. I
care about   think care is volitional and worry is emotional. We must will,
morality   care, choose, decide, love the good—as God does. But we're
without   not to fear or worry. In any case, we've strayed from the point
worrying   again. The point is not which of us is right but simply that our
gurus teach very different things. Jesus the Jew is a moralist.

Huxley: There are Eastern moralists too, you know. Buddha's
Noble Eightfold Path, and the *Dhammapada* . . .

Lewis: But what is the purpose of morality in Eastern religions?

Huxley: To purify the soul of egotistic desire so that it can
see.

Lewis: See what?

Huxley: The truth, the ultimate truth, its own inherent divinity, *tat tvam asi,* "thou art that."

Lewis: But the purpose of morality in the West is to love and
please and obey and praise and glorify God, who wills it.

Huxley: So you try to work your way into heaven, eh?

Lewis: Certainly not. God doesn't save us because we're good,
but we do become good because he saves us. We *want* to; we
love him; it's not an onerous law, or a guilt trip.

Huxley: I think we're digressing again.

Lewis: Yes. The main point is the difference between your
gurus and mine.

Huxley: But morality is pretty much universal the world over,
as you yourself have pointed out in many places, notably *The*

Abolition of Man. The morality of the gurus is the same as the morality of Jesus. The *Dhammapada* and the *Tao Te Ching* teach the same morality as the Sermon on the Mount.

Lewis: Perhaps in content, but not in purpose. We've just seen that difference.

Huxley: All right. Let that pass for now. What's your fifth difference?

Lewis: The fifth point is the most important of all because it deals with the most important question anyone can ask, the question of the purpose of human life, the question "What must I do to be saved?"

(5) What must I do to be saved?

Huxley: All right, what *must* I do?

Lewis: According to Jesus, you must be born again.

Huxley: And what does that mean? Certainly not an emotional high.

Lewis: Of course not. Something deeper than the emotions, something ontological, not just psychological. Being born again means getting a new nature, the divine nature.

Huxley: Aha! So Christianity, like pantheism, teaches that Man is divine. There's the esoteric truth.

Lewis: First of all, it's not esoteric, it's public teaching. Second, it's not that we're all divine by nature but that we must *get* a divine nature. We're born into the world without it, in a state of "original sin," separation from God.

Huxley: Another guilt-producing thought.

Lewis: Only if taken in isolation from salvation, the problem without the solution.

Huxley: The phrase "original sin" is nowhere in the Bible, you know.

Lewis: I know. But the reality it designates certainly is.

Huxley: I beg to differ. There are abundant textual references to our being "children of God." Jesus teaches us to call God our Father.

God is not   *Lewis:* After we become believers and receive the beginning
everyone's   of the divine nature by faith. Before that, we are *not* children
Father.   of God and God is *not* our Father. That's why we have to be
                   born again.

Huxley: But surely God is the Father of all mankind.

Lewis: What do you mean by that?

Huxley: Surely God has universal power and universal justice over mankind.

Lewis: A tyrant, king or parliament can have that. What makes God a *Father?*

Huxley: Surely God loves and cares for all mankind.

Lewis: A nurse or a babysitter can give that. What does a father give that no one else can give? Remember our earlier conversation?

Huxley: Human life.

Lewis: Exactly. Human fathers give human life, animal fathers give animal life, God the Father gives divine life. It's called *grace.*

Huxley: This point of view is quite alien to the great mystics. It takes time and change too seriously, especially the "before" of the "before and after" diptych of sin and salvation.

Lewis: Quod erat demonstrandum. Exactly what I've been trying to prove. Jesus does *not* teach the same thing the gurus teach, especially on this most crucial question of all.

Huxley: I'd like to let that point ride for just a minute—whether

Jesus really taught this . . . this . . . salvationalism . . .

Lewis: Christianity. You wonder whether Christ taught Christianity.

Huxley: No, but let that point go for a minute. I want to see how far you go with the logical consequences of this view. You say we don't have the divine life to begin with?

Lewis: No.

Huxley: And we get it only by believing?

Lewis: Yes.

Huxley: And what happens to those who don't believe?

Lewis: If you do not believe, you will not be saved.

Huxley: So if you don't believe Christianity, you go to hell.

Lewis: The object of faith is not Christianity but Christ. "If you do not believe, you will not be saved" does not mean "If your mind thinks the wrong thoughts, you will go to hell after you die." It means, "If you refuse to accept the offer of divine marriage, you will be spiritually sterile. If you do not let God into your soul, you will not have divine life in your soul." In fact, this is the sixth difference I was going to bring up: the real possibility of hell, of damnation.

Huxley: Back to that damnable doctrine? The hell with hell! **(6) Hell**

Lewis: That's what you say. But it's not what Jesus says. Once again, that's my point: the difference.

Huxley: Jesus couldn't have taught such a terrible thing. It must have been a later accretion, perhaps from that terrible rigorist St. Paul.

Lewis: As a matter of fact, almost all the warnings about hell come from Jesus, and the only passages that offer any kind of hope of a universal salvation come from St. Paul. That's very simply verified just by reading the New Testament. People who repeat that old saw only show what they haven't read.

Huxley: I'll let that pass. But hell seems to stick out like a sore thumb when you consider the rest of Jesus' teachings: love and forgiveness and nonresistance.

Creation plus free will logically entails hell.

Lewis: No, it fits necessarily, if only you grant two background beliefs from Judaism: creation and free will. As soon as you believe in these two things, you must also believe in hell.

Huxley: Prove that. How does that follow?

Lewis: If God created really free persons distinct from himself, they *can* freely choose to remain alienated from him forever. But if the East is right and God never created, if we're all eternally parts of God, then of course there can be no alienation from God, no hell. There can be nothing *but* God.

Huxley: It all hangs together.

Lewis: Yes. Hell is the logical conclusion of sin, of evil. Point six follows from point . . . whichever it was. The one about good and evil.

Huxley: So you believe in God's bloodthirsty vengeance on sinners.

Lewis: No, on *sin*. All sin, all spiritual garbage, necessarily meets its due end, destruction. God can't let garbage into heaven. Only if the sinner won't let go of his garbage does he get burned with it. God offers to take the garbage off his back, to separate the sinner from the sin so that the sinner is not separated from God. Jesus is the garbage man. But if we're too proud to go to the garbage man . . .

Huxley: Excuse me for interrupting your sermon on garbage, but I've just realized that each of your six points is a dualism: ego vs. other, Creator vs. creation, knower vs. known, good vs. evil, divine nature vs. human nature, and heaven vs. hell.

Lewis: Quite so. And you can deny that these dualisms were really part of Jesus' teachings only by inventing *another* dualism, one that isn't there: the dualism between exoteric Christianity, which is Christianity, and esoteric Christianity, which is pantheism. Your esoteric Christianity hasn't a textual syllable to stand on; it's a pure invention, a hypothesis to save a dogma.

Esoteric Christianity, a rationalization for the dogma of the unity of all religions

Huxley: Dogma? What dogma?

Lewis: The dogma of the unity of all world religions. But even if this were true, it couldn't be true in the case of Jesus. To call Jesus a guru contains a built-in self-contradiction even if he *did* have an esoteric teaching which was pantheism.

Huxley: I should know better than to ask, but now seems to be the time to cash in our chips. Our six points are finally coming home to roost in your argument, I see. All right, what is the self-contradiction in my belief that Jesus is the guru to the Jews?

Lewis: It makes Jesus not a guru but a fool. A guru's exoteric teaching is supposed to be a symbolic or mythical version of his esoteric teaching, suitable for the unenlightened masses, is it not?

Huxley: Well, I wouldn't put it quite that way, but something like that.

Lewis: In any case, it's meant to lead them closer to the esoteric teaching, right?

Huxley: Right.

Lewis: But Jesus' exoteric teaching, which we *do* have abundant evidence for in Scripture, led his followers in exactly the wrong direction on all six of these crucial points. In other words, Jesus was so bad a teacher that he couldn't do what any modern writer like yourself could do: say what he meant

If Jesus is a guru, he is a poor one.

so that people would understand him, or at least move them closer to the truth rather than farther away from it. If that's a guru, I'm a goose!

Huxley: That *is* a guru, and if you don't recognize that, you *are* a goose.

Kennedy: Before the goosefeathers fly, has anyone noticed the sky?

Lewis: By Jove, he's right. It's getting brighter.

Huxley: We were so caught up in the argument that we never noticed.

Lewis: Perhaps the light dawning in the argument kept us from noticing the light dawning in the sky.

Kennedy: But did you notice where the dawn seems to be coming from?

Lewis: How strange! From the zenith instead of the horizon.

Huxley: And isn't it strange how we all just assumed that the argument has to be over by sunrise?

Kennedy: Is there any question in your mind?

Huxley: No. I don't know how I know that, but I do.

Lewis: So do I. I think we should spend our last few minutes on the unfinished business that still separates us. Aldous, what is the nub of your defense against my argument?

The textual issue: the nub of the argument

Huxley: Your biblicism, your reliance on the biblical texts. We keep backing into the textual issue and then backing out of it. I want to bail Jack out of your *aut deus aut homo malus* argument by challenging the premise that Jesus claimed to be the unique Son of God, and I want to do that by challenging the historical accuracy of the New Testament texts. How could we deal with that issue now?

Lewis: The issue is quite complicated on the technical textual level, and it has been hotly argued for many years. I don't think we're going to be allowed to review that long argument here. But there is a second aspect to the issue that's seldom considered, and we could question that in a very short time.

Huxley: What aspect?

Lewis: The psychological.

Huxley: We're talking about texts. How do you get off into psychology? That's a diversion.

Lewis: No. It's central. It's human beings that study texts. Human beings have motives.

The motive for maligning the texts

Huxley: But most of the textual study is scientific and objective. Some is even mathematical. Some is computer work. Figures don't lie.

Lewis: No, but liars figure.

Kennedy: He's got you there, Aldous. There's always the human factor.

Lewis: And in fact most modernist biblical criticism has *not* been scientific and objective, as it claims to be. It almost always approaches the text with a priori religious dogmas and unquestioned assumptions in mind, notably, disbelief in miracles. From the psychological point of view the modernist reconstruction of the texts seems suspiciously like fudging the data to fit the a priori theory, altering the evidence, doctoring the tapes.

Huxley: Don't you do the same thing from the opposite direction? You do believe in miracles, so you accept the miracle stories. Why isn't that just as prejudiced?

Lewis: Because the texts *are* miracle stories. I don't add miracles to them; the modernist subtracts them.

Huxley: He thinks the early church added them.

Lewis: And especially Jesus' claim to divinity?

Huxley: Yes. Only because of that claim does your *aut deus aut homo malus* argument work. I say Jesus never claimed divinity, that later writers foisted those words upon him, and I don't see how you could possibly refute that now, two thousand years after the fact.

If Jesus never claimed divinity, the New Testament writers were very stupid or liars.

Lewis: I think it *is* refutable. Consider this: the modernist has to say that the writers of the New Testament were either very stupid or very bad, deliberate liars.

Huxley: This sounds like the *aut deus aut homo malus* argument again. Why the either-or?

Lewis: Because if they thought Jesus claimed to be God when he didn't, they must be very stupid. They were Jews, remember, not Hindus. No one in the world is less likely to confuse the Creator with a creature than a Jew, and he is less likely to confuse Creator with any creature than to confuse any two creatures. The first difference is infinite, the second only finite. On the other hand, if the New Testament writers knew Jesus didn't really claim to be God and they falsified the story to make him say that, then they're not only deliberate liars but they foisted on the world the greatest hoax, the greatest lie, the greatest forgery in all of history.

Huxley: How can you be sure they didn't do just that? You can't cross-examine them two thousand years later. You have no hard evidence.

Lewis: But consider what that hypothesis entails.

Huxley: What?

Lewis: The psychological absurdity of saints living and martyrs dying for a blasphemous, stupid practical joke.

Huxley: Too bad for them, but tragic mistakes happen.

Lewis: But what could possibly have motivated the original creation of the lie? What did its inventors get out of it? Persecuted, exiled, tortured, imprisoned and killed, that's what. People who lie and deceive, especially when the lie is so clever and complete and systematic, always do it for a reason, for a motive, for some personal advantage. Who did it and for what motive?

Huxley: It does seem psychologically unlikely. No, most modernists don't take that line. They don't think the texts were deliberate hoaxes, but myths.

Lewis: That's even more absurd, both literarily and theologically. Literarily because the Gospels simply aren't written as myths but as history. Theologically, because no Jew could possibly confuse Creator and creature so blasphemously.

Kennedy: Lewis, you said you wanted to investigate the psychological angle of the attack on the texts. If the modernist position is as absurd as you make it out to be, what motive do you see behind so many educated people embracing such absurdities?

Lewis: It must be a very strong motive to blissfully wade into such muddy pools of nonsense. I think it must be a religious motive.

Kennedy: A religious motive! I thought it was to *avoid* religion in the traditional sense. These are humanists we're talking about, and by *your* standards humanism is not religious but irreligious.

Lewis: Everyone has some religion, some ultimate. The religion of modern society is egalitarianism, democracy, brotherhood, society itself.

Huxley: You mean conformity.

The religious motive behind modernism: egalitarianism

Lewis: Yes. Being accepted. Being popular. Being one of the community. It's a radically new ideal in the modern West, according to Riesman in *The Lonely Crowd,* but it's just the modern version of a very ancient answer to the question of the ultimate value, or the *summum bonum.* The ancients called it "honor," being respected by others for being superior in some way. We still want the same thing—respect and acceptance by others—but we get it not by being different but by being the same.

Huxley: That point has been made by many observers of modern society: Nietzsche, Kierkegaard, Orwell, Ortega y Gasset . . . even a certain Aldous Huxley. What's the connection with modernist theology?

Christian theology's odium of elitism *Lewis:* The modern world fears elitism, and elitist claims. Now Christian ethics is not as elitist, as distinctive, as Christian theology. Love fits the egalitarian religion of the modern world much better than faith does, if you mean faith in the God of biblical revelation, not just faith in a vague force of your own imagination, or faith in faith. Nearly everyone admits the claims of love, at least in principle if not in practice; but only believers admit the claims of faith.

Huxley: True. Now how does this apply to Jesus?

Lewis: Nearly everyone agrees with Jesus' ethical teachings, because they're very similar to those of Buddha and Lao-Tzu and the others . . .

Huxley: So you admit that he's one of the gurus!

Lewis: As far as his ethics is concerned, yes. But his claim to divinity is unique, and offensive. So if you can only classify Jesus with other ethical teachers and forget the claim to divinity, you're home free with humanism. You can classify Christ with the gurus and Christianity with world religions. You thus remove the odium of distinctiveness, the taint of elitism, the scandal of being right where others are wrong. You satisfy the demands of your god Egalitarianism.

Huxley: Hmmm . . . Whether what you say is true or not, you have certainly given me a puzzle, perhaps a *koan,* certainly food for much thought. I feel I ought to do some more of that—thinking—before I do any more talking with you. For me, at any rate, our dialog seems to have come to an end, perhaps a turning point.

Conclusion: the personal reactions to the argument

Lewis: Perhaps a beginning.

Kennedy: I must confess, Lewis, that you make me feel very uncomfortable, sometimes even angry. Must you make such a judgmental analysis of others' motivations?

Lewis: As I said before, if the shoe fits, wear it. The logical arguments seem so clearly to point against the modernist that one must ask what could have motivated him to embrace such nonsense. What's behind his ingenious attempt to justify the unjustifiable? I want to smoke it out because I suspect that it just might, in many cases, be something much more serious than mere logical fallacy or scholarly error.

Kennedy: What?

Lewis: A spiritual disease.

Kennedy: Careful now! Remember Jesus' advice, "judge not, that you be not judged."

Lewis: I judge myself first of all. I happen to know something about this disease because I have had it. I too am a son of Adam.

Kennedy: What's the disease?

Lewis: Some theologians call it *vincible ignorance.* A less technical term is *dishonesty.* I mean deliberately looking away from or changing the truth when it threatens you.

Honesty: the great difficulty

Kennedy: Are you accusing us of dishonesty? Just because we disagree with you?

Lewis: Certainly not. In fact, I'm overjoyed that both of you seem so open-minded and genuinely curious about this terribly important issue. Nor am I saying that all or most modernists or humanists are dishonest. I'm just playing the prophet and warning you against it.

Huxley: Hadn't you better warn yourself as well?

Lewis: Indeed. I do so repeatedly. In fact, I wrote a poem to that purpose. May I quote it now?

Kennedy: Please do.

Lewis: I dislike quoting my own writing, but this seems to be appropriate now, even though it seems to be almost morning and the poem is called "The Apologist's Evening Prayer."

Huxley: Perhaps both morning and evening are really one, or opposite symbols for the same reality: truth, the light that comes in deepest darkness, the life that comes at the evening point of death.

Lewis: That's very profound, Aldous. Your teachers are not fools, at any rate.

Huxley: Could you quote the poem now?

Lewis: Yes.

"The Apologist's Evening Prayer"

From all my lame defeats and oh! much more
From all the victories that I seemed to score;
From cleverness shot forth on Thy behalf
At which, while angels weep, the audience laugh;
From all my proofs of Thy divinity,
Thou, who wouldst give no sign, deliver me.

Thoughts are but coins. Let me not trust, instead
Of Thee, their thin-worn image of Thy head.

From all my thoughts, even from my thoughts of Thee,
O thou fair Silence, fall, and set me free.
Lord of the narrow gate and the needle's eye,
Take from me all my trumpery lest I die.

Kennedy: Amen to that. Whatever God answers, that's my prayer too.

Huxley: No honest man could quarrel with that. Whatever the outcome of the argument, we must follow the argument in order to follow the truth, and we must follow the truth in order to follow the light.

Lewis: If you really believe that, then we are together in this, in our love of the light.

Kennedy: Look! The light! It is coming!

Huxley: We must follow it. . . . Oh! It's too bright. I never realized how hard it is to follow it. It's like the rising sun.

Kennedy: No, it's . . . it's . . .

Lewis: It's the Rising Son. He is coming!

The Light: Are you coming?

Epilogue

The concluding appeal that Lewis addressed to his two friends is clearly the appeal that God addresses to every rational creature at every moment: the appeal to face truth, to resist the temptation to ignore uncomfortable questions, to overcome the fear of being wrong, to accept life's invitation to grow, to change one's mind and life for the sake of truth, and perhaps even one's nature if the truth is that we must be "born again."

As Lewis says in his poem, our judgment must begin at home. The rarest words to hear from a writer are the words, "I was wrong," especially when the subject is religion. But these are the words *everyone* must speak before God when we meet him. *No* one has God cased. "Eye has not seen, ear has not heard, neither has it entered into the heart of man, what God has prepared for those who love him." Since we all must meet the Light and confess where we were wrong, we'd better get some practice in now, before we meet the Light for the last time.

Whenever we meet him now, whenever new truth shines on old minds, those minds must break to grow. The new wine bursts the old wineskins and requires new wineskins. The new wine is Christ, and the old wineskins are the old earth (which was burst at the Incarnation) and our old self (which is burst at the new birth). It is for that bursting, that spiritual incursion into our being, that "spiritual marriage," that he came. It was for that that we were created. Perhaps it was that for which the entire universe was created. And it is for that that he continually arranges all the events of the universe and of all human lives by his providence—even events as unlikely as logical arguments.

Postscript

It has been over twenty years since I wrote *Between Heaven and Hell,* and my publisher has invited me to explain (1) why and how I came to write it, and perhaps also (2) why it has remained in print so long and has found so many hands into which it has been passed from one reader to another.

As to the second question, I do not think that the answer to that is known to any human author, only to the Author of all authors, who waters and fertilizes the ground (the human need, the "market") and then quietly inspires the farmer (the human author) to sow his seed (the book) on the ground, or, as Ecclesiastes says, to cast his bread upon the waters. (You could call InterVarsity Press the National Breadcasting Company.) There is always a need for apologetics, especially when it combines the logical and the personal, as this book tries to do, and most especially when it focuses on Jesus, as this book does, for he is not only the center of Christianity but also the center of all reality and the meaning and end of all creation. (See Colossians 1.) If he is not that, then Christianity is simply false. As to why this time was (and is) the right time for such a book, I simply do not know. Thoreau says: "Read not the *Times;* read the eternities," and I think that is good advice. The timeless is always timely.

But I can tell you some interesting things about the first question.

I usually take six to twelve months to write a book. I have been working on one (a novel) for nineteen years. But I wrote *Between Heaven and*

Hell in just three days (actually, just three long afternoons), and then spent just three more days revising and polishing it. That's all. It almost wrote itself. When I finished, I sent the manuscript to Christopher Derrick, an English friend, writer and one of C. S. Lewis's students. He wrote back: "I am insanely jealous: this is exactly the book I had planned to write but you got there first."

George Sayer, Lewis's angelic friend and most reliable biographer (his *Jack* is the best of the Lewis bios), met me after he had read my book and asked me how many times I had met Lewis. "Never," I said. "Impossible," he replied. "You make Lewis sound exactly the way he sounded in real life, not just his style of writing but his style of talking. How did you do that?" I have no idea, but it was the best compliment anyone ever gave my writing.

The book emerged suddenly, as an "aha!" experience, when three things converged in my mind: Socratic dialogs, three providentially "coincidental" deaths and three philosophies of life.

First, I had always loved Socrates, and Socratic dialogs, as do nearly all beginning philosophy students. (I'm still a beginner. If I don't know that, I haven't learned lesson one from Socrates. I'm seventy years old, and I still don't know what I want to be when I grow up.) There is simply no philosopher like Socrates and no writer like Plato. It is surely an almost clumsily obvious piece of divine providence that the father of all philosophy, who wrote nothing himself (like Jesus and like Buddha), should have history's greatest philosophical poet, Plato, as his biographer. The first philosophical writer is also the greatest; there has never been another Plato. In forty-five years of teaching, I have tried as many different ways of teaching philosophy as you can imagine, and also some that you can't; but there is simply no better way to teach beginning philosophy, to seduce students into the actual love of wisdom, than to have them read Plato.

I therefore assign to my beginning students the task of imitating this master. (Imitation of a master is a classic, tried and true method of education. The modern cult of originality is simply self-defeating. As C. S. Lewis says, try to be original and you will end up only being foolish. Just be yourself and tell the truth as you see it, and you will end up being original without trying.) And my students always respond well. They enjoy writing Socratic dialogs, and they always do it well. The form is eminently imitable.

I therefore went around asking all the philosophers, philosophy teachers and philosophy writers I knew why no one wrote Socratic dialogs any more, why no one picked up on this engaging form that Plato gave to the world. And I simply got no answers at all! "It's just not done any more," was the consensus. But like a troublesome kid, I wanted to know *why*. (Troublesome kids usually make the best philosophers.) Since neither my peers nor my students could give me any reason for not writing more Socratic dialogs, I decided to find out myself why it couldn't be done by trying it, failing, and learning from my failure.

Twenty years and thirteen books of Socratic dialogs later, I still have not learned. Readers usually like these dialog books best of all. Dialog is simply more interesting than monolog. Putting ideas into people's mouths and into the intellectual equivalent of a battlefield or a prize fighting ring makes them come alive. It adds the concrete, dramatic and personal dimensions to the abstract, logical arguments.

I read in some biography of C. S. Lewis, my favorite author of the last 733 years, that Lewis had tried his hand at some Socratic dialogs too, but never published them, and they were lost when he died. They probably perished in the first day of the bonfire that his brother Warnie made of his unpublished manuscripts after he died, in an attempt to be faithful to the intentions of his brother, before Walter Hooper arrived on the scene the next day and rescued the rest of them. This made me even more determined to do it. My favorite author had tried it, but we would never know the results.

I had just finished *Heaven, the Heart's Deepest Longing,* which is my favorite of all the fifty-plus books I have written, and I wrote that also because of Lewis. Lewis never wrote a book-length treatment of the theme that is certainly the most moving, arresting and unique in all of his writing, the mysterious desire he calls "Joy" or *Sehnsucht;* so I had to do it myself. I write the books I want to read. I wish someone else had written them, but they didn't, so if I'm going to read these books, I have to write them first.

Second, Lewis died the same day as John F. Kennedy (November 22, 1963), in fact almost the same hour (early afternoon). Thus, few noticed his passing, just as few noticed the death of the most beloved Christian of modern times, Mother Teresa of Calcutta, because she died at the same time as Princess Diana. When I think of her quiet death and the reason it was unnoticed, I cannot help thinking of how St. Paul was drowned out by the pagans in Ephesus shouting, "Great is Diana of the Ephesians!" I wonder: is there a deliberate providential pattern there?

I had known that Lewis and Kennedy died the same day, but I discovered, on the very same Monday that I discovered that Lewis's Socratic dialogs had perished in the bonfire, that Aldous Huxley had also died that same afternoon. I knew Huxley from his great novel *Brave New World,* one of the two most prophetic books of the twentieth century, the other being C. S. Lewis's *The Abolition of Man.* But I also knew him from his engaging anthology of world mysticism, *The Perennial Philosophy,* a book whose whole point is, as Chesterton put it, that "Buddhism and Christianity are really the same, especially Buddhism."

The three deaths were as different as the three lives had been, and providentially perfect templates of the three philosophies of life that had motivated them. Kennedy was murdered by an assassin; for he who lives by politics may die by politics, as "he who lives by the sword will die by the sword" (Matthew 26:52). Huxley died of an LSD overdose while experimenting with mystical experience; for he who lives by man-made mysticisms will die by man-made mysticisms. Lewis died of bone disease, a few years after he had taken the pain of his dying wife's bone cancer out of her body and into his, beside her bedside; for he who lives by the Way of Exchange will die by the Way of Exchange. Like Christ, he offered God his own life for hers, and on November 22, God accepted the offer.

We do not choose to die or not to die. But we choose *how* to die, and it is congruent with and a consequence of how we choose to live. The One who tells the story that includes all lives set before our eyes—these three lives and these three deaths—with a clarity and a coinciding that was no coincidence.

Third, I had written a short essay years earlier on what I think are the three most basic worldview options, or philosophies of life, in the world: ancient Eastern religion (essentially, pantheism or monism), ancient Western religion (theism, especially Christianity), and modern irreligion or secularism. When these three things came together in my mind, on a certain Monday, *Between Heaven and Hell* was instantly conceived. For these three men were famous, classic and clever representatives of these three worldviews. It was as if God had set it up, "jimmying" things so that these three could meet and have a Socratic dialog in the next world on the meaning of life.

And since Jesus is the answer to that question for Lewis, and for all Christians, the dialog centered around not just three abstract philosophies, like my essay, but three views of Jesus, three answers to the most momentous question there is, if Christianity is true: "What think ye of Christ?" (Matthew 22:42). What happens when you touch your mind to the cosmic touchstone?

Perhaps something like this dialog might happen. *Between Heaven and Hell* arose from the same kind of "supposition" as Lewis's Narnia chronicles (if the reader can excuse me for comparing my mouse of amateur apologetics with Lewis's elephant of the greatest children's stories of all time). In writing the Narnia books Lewis did not set out to write an allegory (how could Tolkien have missed that fact?) but a "thought experiment": suppose Jesus came in a different form (lion) to a different world (Narnia)? What might happen? Similarly, I did not set out to write a logical argument, to merely dress up the classical "Lord, liar, or lunatic" argument with new Socratic clothing, but to imagine what might actually happen if these three real men met after death and talked to each other. The difference between the two thought experiments, Lewis's and mine, is that Lewis did not really think it was probable that there was a real world called Narnia and that Jesus went there as a lion, but I know it is true that there is a real world in the next life and that we go there and that we communicate with each other (for the "communion of saints" is not limited to this world alone), so I think it is really quite possible, even probable, that these three men actually had some such conversation. It is, of course, purely an imaginative supposition, not a claim to know the unknowable. But if our roots are grounded in God's certain truth, why should we not stretch the leaves and branches of our imagination far into the uncertain heavens? Is not man a tree rather than a worm?

In addition to this postscript, I have also added to the original book a little imaginative dialog which takes place in the present time and place but in an alternative world, a world in which Jesus never rose from the dead. It is called "A World Without an Easter" and is about the difference Jesus made and continues to make to our world.

Appendix A

A World Without an Easter

Mara, a young woman with a bitter, sorrowful, washed-out look, is walking through the snow on a city street, carrying a small evergreen tree. She accidentally bumps into Rabbi Nathan, since both are looking down, sheltering their faces from the winter wind. Rabbi Nathan is old but sprightly, and wears a yarmulke.

Mara: Oh, excuse me, sir. I didn't mean to bump into you. Are you all right?

Rabbi Nathan: Oh, quite all right, thank you, child. It's no wonder you didn't see me. How can you see from behind that tree you're carrying? What in the world are you doing with *that?* It looks awfully heavy for a woman to carry. Would you like some help? Here, let my slave carry it for you.

M (surprised): Oh . . . why, thank you, kind sir.

RN: You're carrying that all by yourself. Where is *your* slave?

M: Oh, we're too poor to have any.

RN: Not even one slave? Oh, you poor woman. How can you get anything done without good slaves?

M: Oh, we manage. But I don't understand—why do you go out of your way to help me? What am I to you?

RN: A stranger in need.

M: That's a most remarkable thing to say in this dog-eat-dog world. Are you—are you a Christian by any chance?

RN: No, I'm a Jew. A rabbi, in fact.

M: Oooh. I don't think I've ever met one of you before. How many of you are left in New Rome?

RN: Since the last pogrom, about six thousand. But we are destined to last until the end of time, you know.

M: I know. You are the True God's Chosen People.

RN: You are one of the few that knows us. What was that sect that you thought I was part of?

M: Christians. I thought you were a Christian.

RN: Are *you* a Christian?

M: Yes.

RN: I think I have never met a Christian before. I remember reading about you people long ago in some old history book. You consider yourself some sort of Jewish sect, don't you?

M: In a way. We believe your scriptures, but we also believe in Jesus of Nazareth as the Messiah, the promised one. We call him the "Christ," the anointed one.

RN: And how many of *you* are there left in New Rome?

M: Not many.

RN: And elsewhere in the world?

M: None, I think.

RN: There are a few Jews in almost every country in the world. We're still the world's troublemakers. Everybody hates us. We're the world's troubled conscience.

M: I know. The world doesn't hate us much, I think. They've just forgotten us, because they have forgotten him.

RN: Who?

M: Jesus.

RN: The man you say was the Messiah?

M: Yes. We still keep his memory. This tree, here, that I was carrying—that's for a festival we celebrate each year, the festival of his birth. We call it "Christmas." We decorate trees with lights and we give gifts to each other.

RN: How quaint! I never heard of that before. It sounds a little like our feast of Hannukah. Say . . . I wonder if you have a few minutes free to talk to an old man about things I don't know. I'm always eager to learn about strange new customs and beliefs.

M: All right. What do you want to know?

RN: *Why* do you keep his memory?

M: Because memory is a precious thing.

RN: Oh, I know that, all right. But why do you single him out and call him the Messiah? Wasn't he crucified as a criminal about two thousand years ago?

M: So the old stories say. But who knows what happened, really? Some of us hope that he somehow escaped death. There are strange rumors . . .

RN: Where is he now, then, if he escaped death?

M: Nobody knows. The few records we have are uncertain. They're just paper, after all. And there is no one alive with the authority to say what really happened.

RN: So you don't have divinely authorized scriptures like ours? Detailed eyewitness accounts of great prophets like Abraham and Moses and David?

M: No.

RN: I suppose you wouldn't have scriptures about him if he ended his life as a condemned criminal. But how then can you say he was the Messiah?

M: He said so himself.

RN: Why do you believe him?

M: Because we believe he was the wisest man who ever lived.

RN: And why do you believe that?

M: Because of the teachings we have from him.

RN: Where are these teachings to be found?

M: They were passed down by word of mouth and written down generations later.

RN: Oh, I think I remember now. He preached a great sermon, didn't he? You call it the "Sermon on the Mount," don't you?

M: Yes.

RN: Those are some very beautiful sayings. But didn't this Jesus also predict that he would rise from the dead? Or am I confusing him with some other forgotten old myth?

M: Yes, he did predict that.

RN: It must have been quite a disappointment to his followers when he didn't do what he predicted.

M: Oh, but we believe that he really did rise from the dead, in the only really important sense.

RN: Really, you mean? Literally? Bodily?

M: No, spiritually. He rose from the dead in our hearts. We celebrate the feast of his resurrection too. We call it Easter.

RN: What do you do on Easter?

M: We have chicks and bunnies and eggs, as symbols of new life.

RN: Why do you celebrate a resurrection feast for Jesus if Jesus didn't really rise?

M: What rose from the dead was Easter faith.

RN: Faith in what? How can there be Easter faith unless Easter really happened?

M: It was our mistake to take his prediction literally, of course. But it was still a profound symbol. The rising really happened, but not in a stone tomb. It happened in us: in our hearts and minds and lives.

RN: I'm sorry to say this—I know it must sound cynical to you but that sounds like the pagan nonsense we Jews rejected many, many centuries ago. The pagans had corn gods and vegetation gods aplenty, you know—they still do—and if you ask them when these gods lived, the answer is always something like yours. They say the god rises from the dead every year when the earth awakens in the spring, or when their hearts celebrate the feast of spring. You see, that's what's so different about us, about Jews: we know the real deeds of God in the world, in history. We don't believe in vague, abstract, spiritual symbols of ourselves or our world; we believe in the real God who acted in history. He performed miracles. They were visible. If your Jesus doesn't fit that pattern, you can't claim that you are any kind of offshoot of Judaism.

If your Jesus had really risen from the grave, now, you would have had a real event to remember instead of just another vague pagan symbol. But I should be listening to you instead of talking. I'm here to learn, not to lecture. I'm not trying to argue you out of your religion or into mine.

M: Why not, if you believe yours is true?

RN: Because we Jews are not meant to prosyletize, to convert the world, until the true Messiah comes. When that happens, then the whole world will learn of the true God, and the people that lived in darkness will see a great light, and the knowledge of God will extend from sea to sea.

M: We believe that Jesus was that Messiah.

RN: How did he show the world the true God?

M: He called God his Father. He said strange things like "I and the Father are one" and "He who has seen me, has seen the Father."

RN: That sounds blasphemous. Isn't that why he was crucified?

M: Well, we don't really know how to interpret those mysterious sayings of his. Each of us is free to make up our own mind. We are not bound by any authoritative scripture or church.

RN: Your words sound like praise, but your tone sounds like blame. I wonder whether you are bragging or complaining.

M: You're right, Rabbi. You see into my heart. I wish we *did* have some sure teaching authority. It all seems so uncertain, so wispy. Yet there's something wonderful and unforgettable about that man, something . . . something that seems on the verge of *breaking through,* but not quite, if you know what I mean. It's hard to explain. There seems to be something about the stories about him, even if they're only myths, that sets him apart from every other man in history. For instance, no one has ever succeeded in writing convincing fiction about him. Isn't that remarkable? There are legends that say he really performed miracles.

RN: If he really performed miracles, why didn't he perform the big one and rise from the dead?

M: I told you, he rises every time we remember him.

RN: Pious gobbledygook! If he didn't really rise from the dead, you can't raise him by remembering what didn't happen!

M: But isn't *your* tradition full of legends of miracles too? The stories about Moses, for instance . . .

RN: They're not legends. They're history. They really happened.

M: Then why did they stop happening? Why haven't there been miracles happening for the last two thousand years either for Jews or for Christians? Why the power shortage?

RN: That's a very good question. There does seem to have been a power shortage. Different rabbis give different answers to that question, but frankly, none of them has ever quite satisfied me. I just don't know.

M: I don't think miracles ever did happen, even in the past.

RN: You sound bitter when you say that.

M: I guess I am. I wish very hard that miracles really happened. And I wish even harder that God would do some of them today. If the stories about Jesus casting out demons were true, and if Jesus had really risen from the dead, then he could do the same thing today. And that would take care of those Satanists who are taking over the world.

RN: Hush, child! The walls have ears. The Satanists are everywhere nowadays. And we are the two groups they hate the most. Yes, I feel as you do: if only we had the kind of power the Satanists have . . . We have no protection from them.

M: The laws protect us from them. We have to trust in the laws.

RN: The laws! Hmph! The laws of New Rome are only as good as the emperor who enforces them, and he enforces them only when it suits him. God's laws are the only ones you can trust, because God always enforces them.

M: But why did God let things slide so badly out of control in the world then? How could he let his world decay and his people diminish like this? Why, we two are just about the only two groups of people in the world who know the true God, and we're a tiny minority. When will the rest of the world ever learn?

RN: When the Messiah comes.

M: We believe he has come already.

RN: Then why didn't he set things right if he was the true Messiah? Look how bad things have been since the time of Jesus. Ancient Greece and Rome were the last really civilized societies the world has ever had, and the Dark Ages have lasted sixteen centuries now. Will we ever regain the ancient glory?

M: Well? Will we?

RN: When the Messiah comes.

M: And when he comes, what do you believe he will do?

RN: He will establish the kingdom of God.

M: Will the Messiah depose the emperor? Will he enter politics?

RN: Most of us think so. That is one theory. Another is that he will be a spiritual leader, a holy man, a wise man.

M: Jesus was a holy man and a wise man.

RN: But he didn't establish a kingdom, did he?

M: No.

RN: Then how can he be the Messiah?

M: Are you trying to convert me out of my religion?

RN: Are you afraid to ask questions about it?

M: Why do you rabbis always answer a question with another question?

RN: Why *shouldn't* a rabbi answer a question with another question?

M: Ha! You Jews seem to be the only people in the world with a sense of humor. Why is that?

RN: We are God's chosen people.

M: And God is a comedian?

RN: Indeed. Have you ever looked straight at an ostrich?

M: Seriously, how do you keep your sense of humor in such a world as this?

RN: It is our survival trick.

M: No, seriously, Rabbi, how do you cope with what you called the power shortage—*God's* power shortage?

RN: When the Messiah comes, God will put forth his power.

M: So you believe that the Messiah will depose the emperor?

RN: I personally do not think so. I think that the greatest power in the world is holiness, not politics.

M: That sounds like something Jesus would have said. And something the Satanists would laugh at. And so would the emperor.

RN: God will have the last laugh.

M: Do you think he will laugh in scorn?

RN: No, I think he will laugh in love.

M: Love?

RN: Not the love that is sweet feelings, but the love that is self-sacrifice. That is the greatest power.

M: How can self-sacrifice be the greatest *power?*

RN: Didn't your own master Jesus say something like that?

M: Yes, but I never understood it. I guess that's because I never *saw* it. If he were only alive, maybe we would be able to see it still today. But his story ended with defeat and death, just like ours. And not just death but crucifixion. (Bitterly:) That's what happens to love: it gets crucified by power.

RN: No, child. That is not the last word. Love is stronger than hate. Good is stronger than evil. God is stronger than Satan.

M: Then why does the story of the good man end with death? If love is stronger than evil, why isn't love stronger than death?

RN: When the Messiah comes, God will conquer even death, and the righteous dead will rise.

M: When the Messiah comes! When the Messiah comes! You keep harping on that. You pin all your hopes on this mythical figure.

RN: I thought *you* pinned your hopes on him too, and I thought you believed that he was not a mythical figure but a real historical person, this Jesus of yours.

M: He is our ideal.

RN: But not your power source?

M: What do you mean?

RN: He preached that beautiful "Sermon on the Mount," didn't he? About loving your enemies and turning the other cheek, and poverty and even persecution being blessed?

M: Yes.

RN: So how do you expect to have the power to practice that high and holy way of life?

M: We don't. It's our ideal. We strive toward it, as we strive toward the stars.

RN: And you have about as much hope of attaining that ideal as you have of getting to the stars. Your ideal is very much like the stars: the stars are very beautiful but they are so high and far away that they give little light for our daily walk on this earth.

M: But what else can we do? All we can do is to try, and do our best. How can God expect more than that?

RN: But *do* you do your best? Do any of us?

M: You ask such piercing questions! To answer you honestly, no, we don't do our best. We wouldn't feel guilty if we did. So tell me, Rabbi, do you think these high ideals are worthless, then?

RN: Not at all. I believe *God* gave us those high ideals.

M: But they are too high for our power.

RN: Exactly. We can live them only with *his* power.

M: But how do we get *that?*

RN: Somehow, God has to get inside us, not just outside us.

M: And how can *that* happen?

RN: When the Messiah comes, it is said that he will put God's Spirit into our hearts.

M: The Messiah again!

RN: Do you have any better answer to the problem of evil?

M: No. God and goodness seem so distant. We struggle with evil—our own evil and the evil of our enemies—and we always lose. How can we ever win?

RN: I think I saw a little glimmer of light in answer to that just today, when I was in prayer and asking God that very question. I asked him: "Why do I always fail? Is it my fault or yours?" And I held up both hands as I said it, like this (holds up both hands), as if my left hand was myself and my right hand was God. And I think I got an answer to my question.

M: You mean God *spoke* to you?

RN: No, not in words. But there was a sign. My two hands came together, like this (moves hands slowly together), without my conscious effort. I took that as a sign, and as my answer: If God and we somehow came together, we could conquer evil, starting with the evil inside our souls, our own sins. But he *will* not do it without us, and we *cannot* do it without him. He will not do it without us because of our freedom, and we cannot do it without him because of our bondage.

M: That is very profound.

RN: But it is not enough. Because the problem remains: *how* do we get together? It is easy for my two hands to come together, but how can the immortal God and mortal man come together? My only answer is hope: hope that when the Messiah comes, God will put his own Spirit inside us. The Messiah will solve the problem.

M: But that's what we believe Jesus did! He and God . . . he was so close to God that he called him his Father.

RN: But how can *you* get so close to God? How can you call God your Father?

M: He is the answer to that question, somehow.

RN: How?

M: We don't know. He solves it somehow.

RN: If your Messiah is dead, how can he do anything? How can a corpse change your life? How can a dead man give new life to the living?

M: He lived the ideal life, and we cherish his memory.

RN: Why do you cherish the memory of an ideal that tortures you because it is unattainable?

M: You're right, it does torture us. But it also inspires us. I have a picture of it in my mind that I can't quite define, but it won't go away. A picture of a new life. I know this is the answer, but I don't know the way to it.

RN: Didn't your Jesus say once, "I am the way"?

M: Yes.

RN: Well, what did he mean by that? How could the *way* be a *man?*

M: I never understood that. Yet I've always been haunted by it, as if it were something hovering teasingly close, just out of reach. I think the answer is somewhere in that legend about Jesus rising from the dead. If only he had risen from the dead, if only he were still alive, if only he were still really present—that would solve *everything.*

RN: But he didn't, and he isn't, and he can't.

M: How do you Jews solve the problem of evil?

RN: Well, we distinguish the thing itself, its cause and its result. The thing itself is our own sins. The cause is our separation from God. And the result is God's just punishment.

M: I didn't mean how you solve the problem of *defining* evil. I meant how you *deal* with it.

RN: We hope in God's forgiveness.

M: And how do you obtain that?

RN: We used to have temple sacrifices, before the Romans destroyed the second temple.

M: You slaughtered animals, didn't you?

RN: Yes.

M: Why?

RN: Because "without the shedding of blood, there is no remission of sins."

M: But the temple no longer exists.

RN: No. So now we live in hope. Hope that when the Messiah comes . . .

M: The Messiah again!

RN: Yes. We are a very concrete, historical people. We do not hope in ideals, we hope in persons. Beginning with God himself.

M: But aren't you afraid to meet him?

RN: Of course. "The fear of the Lord is the beginning of wisdom."

M: I'm afraid to meet him too.

RN: At death, you mean?

M: Yes. First of all, I'm not even sure there *is* any life after death. The only evidence for it is abstract philosophical arguments. No one has ever come back from the dead.

RN: This is true, alas.

M: And then, even if there *is* life after death, how can we be sure God will forgive us for our sins and take us to heaven? What is my entrance ticket? I wish I knew. Life is hard, but death is even harder, isn't it? But tell me, Rabbi, how do you Jews face death? You seem to do it better than anyone. You've been persecuted and tortured and martyred for thousands of years. I'm puzzled by two things about you: how do you endure life, and how do you endure death? What is your secret?

RN: It is not our secret, it is God's secret. We are his chosen people. He gives us special graces to endure, until . . .

M: Until the Messiah comes!

RN: Yes.

M: Well, I envy you. You are a sign of hope to this whole bitter world.

I just wish I had some idea of what to hope for. It's got to be something stronger than death. Something *has* to be stronger than death.

RN: God is stronger than death.

M: Yes, but how do we plug into God? It's easy for God to conquer death, but it's impossible for us. Unless . . . unless God somehow connects us up to him, or connects himself down to us. If only Jesus had risen from the dead! Then *he* would be the link, the man with divine power, the man with . . . the man with a divine nature, if that is possible . . .

RN: Hush, child! You speak blasphemy. And foolishness as well. Myth and moonshine, all this talk about a man rising from the dead. Come on, let's struggle home. We don't have time for such impossible dreams. We have to put one foot in front of the other. Here, let my slave carry your tree—and also that other package you are carrying. What is that, by the way?

M: It's what we put on the tree for Christmas. It's frankincense and myrrh.

RN: Burial spices! Why?

M: We like to preserve his memory. That's our secret of living.

RN: Poor soul! You seek the living among the dead!

If the bones of the dead Jesus were discovered tomorrow in a Palestinian tomb, all the essentials of Christianity would remain unchanged.
Rudolf Bultmann

If Christ has not been raised, then our preaching is vain and your faith is in vain. . . . If Christ has not been raised, your faith is futile and you are still in your sins. Then also those who have fallen asleep in Christ have perished. If for this life only we have hoped in Christ, we are of all men most to be pitied.
St. Paul

Appendix B

Outline to Between Heaven and Hell

The following is meant to be an outline of the logical structure of the argument. The running sidebars in the text also aid the reader in announcing new topics.

This book can be seen either as a confrontation among three worldviews: Christian theism (Lewis), Eastern pantheism (Huxley) and modern Western humanism (Kennedy), or as a defense of the central, unique claim of Christianity (that Jesus Christ is God incarnate) against both modern Western secular objections and ancient Eastern religious objections.

I. Lewis vs. Kennedy
   A. Kennedy's objections (note Lewis's replies to each one)
      1. "new Christianity" vs. "old Christianity"
      2. "Christian values" vs. Christ
      3. Jesus as "man become God" vs. Jesus as God become man
      4. Objection to miracles and the supernatural
      5. Objection to (and misunderstanding of) authority
      6. Objection to "black-and-white thinking"
      7. Objection to "objective truth"
      8. Objection to proofs in religion

   B. The argument: four ways to put the same basic argument
      1. Jesus is *aut deus aut homo malus* (either God or a bad man).
      He is not a bad man.
      Therefore he is God.

Proof of the first premise: A mere man who claims to be God is a bad man, not a good man. He is either a liar (if he doesn't believe his claim) or a lunatic (if he does).

Thus Jesus is either "Lord, Liar or Lunatic."

2. Sages (the wise) are trustable.

Jesus is a sage.

Therefore Jesus is trustable.

And trustable people tell the truth, especially about themselves.

Therefore Jesus tells the truth, especially about himself.

But Jesus says he is God.

Therefore it is true that he is God.

3. How can we classify Jesus?

	Sages (wise, loving and creative):	Non-sages:
All the people who claim to be God (the God of the Bible):	Jesus only	the insane: the "divinity complex"
All the people who do not:	Socrates, Buddha, Moses, Lao-Tzu, Confucius, Muhammad, Solomon, etc.	99.99999% of all humans

Reasons for classifying Jesus as a sage:

a. practical wisdom *(prajna)*, insight into the human heart and character

b. practical love, altruism, compassion *(karuna)*, selflessness, charity

c. creativity, unpredictability, interestingness, multidimensionality, unclassifiability

Lunatics have exactly the opposite three characteristics: platitudinous, egotistic and boring

4. What are all the possibilities about Jesus?

a. He didn't ever claim to be God as the Gospels say: Jesus is a MYTH

    b. He did claim to be God.

        i. By "God" he meant Brahman (the God of Hinduism): Jesus is a GURU

        ii. By "God" he meant YHWH (the God of Judaism)

          1. The claim is false

            a. He knew it was false: Jesus is a LIAR

            b. He didn't know it was false: Jesus is a LUNATIC

          2. The claim is true: Jesus is the LORD

II. Lewis vs. Huxley

A. First objection: Jesus never claimed to be God; the texts are not to be trusted.

Lewis's answers:

1. There is *much textual evidence* for the Jesus of the Gospels and none against it; no evidence for any earlier, original, merely human Jesus, and no evidence for a later dating of the texts that claim divinity or miracles.

2. There is *no motivation* for the invention of the "lie" of a divine Jesus; those who taught it gained nothing by it and lost everything.

3. There is *not enough time* to have a legend of a divine Jesus arise and be believed, for eyewitnesses of the real Jesus would still be alive to contradict the new legend of Jesus.

4. Christianity is *not like any other myth.*

    a. If it is a lie, it is the biggest lie ever told.

    b. The style of the Gospels is realistic eyewitness description, not myth (compare real mythic writings); if it is not true, the apostles invented the modern literary genre of realistic fantasy eighteen centuries ago.

5. If Jesus did not claim to be God, the "liar or lunatic" argument can be applied to whoever invented the "legendary" claim of the divine Jesus:

a. If they believed that Jesus really did claim to be God when in fact he never did claim that, then they were very stupid. Not likely for Jews to confuse God with a man!

b. If they knew Jesus didn't really claim to be God, they were the greatest liars in history—and to what purpose? What advantage? Martyrdom does not prove truth, but it proves sincerity.

B. Second objection: Jesus may have claimed to be God, and in fact was God, but so are all of us. Jesus was a Hindu-type guru, a pantheistic mystic. Jesus was "the guru to the Jews," but both his friends and his enemies failed to understand his true, inner, mystical, esoteric meaning, fastening instead onto his external, literal, exoteric, public words.

Lewis's answers:

1. Christianity, like Judaism, is an exoteric, public, open religion, not an esoteric one.

2. Jesus taught theism, not pantheism. He was a Jew, not a Hindu.

3. If he tried to teach the so-called perennial philosophy of pantheism, he was the least successful teacher of it in history, for he explicitly contradicted it on at least six points:

a. God is personal ("I AM"), not impersonal.

b. God is the transcendent Creator, other and distinct from nature. Nature is neither God nor illusion, as it is in pantheism.

c. God is knowable by divine revelation in visible deeds and written words. Religion is God's search for man, not just man's search for God.

d. God is *good,* not evil and not "beyond good and evil." He has a will and gave a law.

e. Jesus taught sin and salvation; that we do not have divine life by nature, but must receive it from God by grace.

f. Those who do not accept this gift by faith will not be saved; there is hell, because there is created free will.

Index